THE SCANDAL
OF THE
FABLIAUX

THE SCANDAL
OF THE
FABLIAUX

R. HOWARD BLOCH

THE UNIVERSITY OF CHICAGO PRESS
CHICAGO AND LONDON

R. HOWARD BLOCH is chairman of the
Department of French at the University of
California, Berkeley. He is the author of
*Etymologies and Genealogies: A Literary
Anthropology of the French Middle Ages*,
also published by the University of
Chicago Press, and *Medieval French
Literature and Law*.

The University of Chicago Press, Chicago 60637
The University of Chicago Press, Ltd., London
© 1986 by The University of Chicago
All rights reserved. Published 1986
Printed in the United States of America

95 94 93 92 91 90 89 88 87 86   5 4 3 2 1

The general argument and portions of chapter 1
first appeared as "The Fabliaux, Fetishism,
and Freud's Jewish Jokes" in *Representations*,
no. 4 (Fall 1983): 1–26. © 1983 by the
Regents of the University of California

Library of Congress Cataloging-in-Publication Data

Bloch, R. Howard.
  The scandal of the fabliaux.

  Includes index.
    1. Fabliaux—History and criticism.   2. French
poetry—To 1500—History and criticism.   3. Tales—
France—History and criticism.   I. Title.
PQ207.B56   1986   841'.1'09   85-16428
ISBN 0-226-05975-8
ISBN 0-226-05976-6 (pbk.)

This book is dedicated to my parents,
Bertram H. and Virginia R. Bloch

CONTENTS

ACKNOWLEDGMENTS

It is, of course, impossible to thank all those whose intellectual influence and support went into the making of this book; nor, given its controversial nature (which some have compared to the quick and dirty temper of the fabliaux), would they necessarily be anxious to be claimed. Let me, then, simply acknowledge collectively the students who participated in my seminars on the fabliaux at the University of California, Berkeley and at Yale as well as the group around *Representations*; their persistent attention to conceptual coherence as well as to detail has served as a caution throughout. Special thanks are also due Katharine Streip, who husbanded the typescript in its final phase, and to Leo Löwenthal whose own capacity for humor has only improved with age.

INTRODUCTION

Si l'on commence par poser résolument en principe ou
en fait que notre littérature du moyen âge, nos *Chansons
de geste* elles-mêmes, nos *Fabliaux* ou *Fableaux*, nos *Mys-
tères* aussi n'ont aucune valeur littéraire, alors, mais seule-
ment alors, il devient aisé de s'entendre;—et peut-être y
a-t-il moyen d'en dire des choses assez intéressantes.

BRUNETIÈRE

A curious and unnerving quality pervades the encounter be-
tween the King of England and the Jongleur of Ely in the
fabliau by the same name. Curious because one rarely catches
so profound a glimpse of the conditions surrounding poetic
performance in the Middle Ages and, in particular, of the rela-
tion between poetry and political power.[1] Unnerving because
the dialogue between the inquisitive king and the clever poet
turns around three questions that not only continue to fasci-
nate literary specialists, but that indeed have dominated vir-
tually all that has been written about the fabliaux since their
rediscovery and edition in the eighteenth century.

The king's first question—"Dont vien tu?"—is essentially
that of origins. Since the Comte de Caylus's *Mémoire sur les
fabliaux* (1753), scholars have doggedly asked the question of
where the fabliaux come from, a question less interesting in
itself than the history of the attempt to displace the sources of
this anticlerical, antifeminist, and scandalous corpus as far
from Europe and as far from the present as possible. The
fabliaux are perceived to be from a distant time, so distant in
fact that one early student (P. Philippe de la Brennellerie) af-
firmed their origin to be simultaneous with the "creation of
the world." Most of all, the fabliaux are perceived to be geo-
graphically remote. De Caylus roots them in Classical Antiq-
uity, though he admits that twelfth- and thirteenth-century
poets had little knowledge of the appropriate Greek or Latin
texts.[2] His suggestion that they may also have had a distant In-
dian source spawned what remains a rich and respected critical

tradition attempting to trace the fabliaux to an original body of Sanskrit.

The association of the fabliaux with the European folktale and the ascription of both to Ancient India's first centuries of Buddhism is one element of nineteenth-century Orientalism. Thus Silvestre de Sacy, in a book whose title is already half its thesis, claims that "toutes les règles de la saine critique assurent à l'Inde l'honneur d'avoir donné naissance à ce recueil d'apologues, qui fait, encore aujourd'hui, l'admiration de l'Orient et de l'Europe elle-même."[3] Theodor Benfey, whose 600-page Introduction to the German translation of the *Pantchatantra* is a scholarly artifact worthy of study in its own right, asserts, "Wir werden aber weiter sehen, dass gerade der Buddhismus der ganz eigentliche Träger von Fabeln und Märchen ist."[4] Benfey's notion that we will not understand European folktales until we have reduced all—"or almost all"—to their Indian prototype represents an attempt to retrace what Gaston Paris will later refer to as the "long caravan of tales stretching from the banks of the Ganges to the Seine."[5] Nor will the water imagery be lost on Ten Brink, whose description of the fable's long journey "from India to the Atlantic Ocean, singly and in collections, orally and in writing," is a masterpiece of imprecision.[6]

One finds an even further displacement in the so-called Aryan explanation, first espoused by the Brothers Grimm (1856), according to which the fabliaux are merely the final stages in the evolution of ancient solar, stellar, and crepuscular myths born among the Indo-European people before their division into Slavic, German, Latin, Celtic, Iranian, and Indian groups. The European folktale is, for the Grimms, Adalbert Kuhn, Michel Bréal, and Max Müller, the ultimate degradation of a prehistoric heroic mythos transformed into legends; and legends, under the pressure of Christianity, transformed into tales.[7] Thus the route back to India is not far enough. The Aryanists propose to return the fable to "that distant age before any Greek had put foot in Europe and before any Hindu had bathed in the sacred waters of the Ganges"; that failing, to that time, described by Müller with the vividness of a witness, "when nursemaids under the peasant roofs of Norway, the elms of Thuringia, the enormous fig-trees of India all told similar tales."[8]

Following the lead of comparative philologists, both the Orientalists and the Aryanists equate chronology with cause, which takes them into the dicey area of analogy between linguistics and race. And just as the historical linguists of the nineteenth century sometimes confused grammar with blood—"the blood which circulates in their grammar is Arian blood" (Müller)—early writers on the fabliaux tended to attribute them to (or blame them on) the Arabs and the Jews.[9] Benfey, writing in 1859, asserts that the Jews were the principal intermediaries between the Arabs and the French and that they introduced a "disproportionate number of Oriental fables to Western Europe."[10] Much of Benfey's argument is based on the fact that the *Disciplina clericalis*, a twelfth-century Latin collection with clear sources in Eastern wisdom literature, was translated into Old French. The author of the *Disciplina clericalis*, Petrus Alfonsi, was himself a converted Jew whose warnings to those who are "intellectually lazy" and who are "too proud of their status as teachers to play the role of pupil"[11] might well have served the editor of the *Recueil général des fabliaux* (1872), Anatole de Courde de Montaiglon, who maintains that "les premiers sont les Arabes, mais ils n'eussent pas suffi; le second et vrai intermédiaire, c'est le peuple cosmopolite par excellence, et le seul qui le fut au moyen âge, c'est-à-dire, les Juifs, orientaux eux-mêmes d'esprit et de tradition, qui seuls savaient l'arabe et qui seuls pouvaient le traduire en latin, la langue unique et générale par le canal de laquelle un conte aussi bien qu'une idée pourrait entrer dans le courant européen" (*Recueil*, I, xvii). The true source of the fabliaux is supposedly the Talmud by which the Jews gave to Europe "et le thème et la matière." All of which de Courde de Montaiglon asserts, in a supremely aristocratic intellectual gesture, without the slightest knowledge of Hebrew: "Il serait digne d'un hébraïsant érudit de s'attacher à ce filon et d'en établir l'importance" (*Recueil*, I, xviii). Thus, speculation about the roots of the fabliaux not only lends itself to Romantic fantasy but from the start can be considered a phenomenon of reception by projection.

The King of England's second question—"ou qy este vus?"—is that of the fabliaux's so-called historical or sociological realism. Because these tales seem to contain a more rounded spectrum of social types than the epic, the lyric, or the romance, because they exhibit tradesmen, clerics, peasants, as well as knights and nobles, and because the vision of human nature they portray appears on the surface closer to a kind of grasping materialism than to the idealism of courtly forms, scholars traditionally have concluded that the fabliaux offer a privileged view of the way things really were in the thirteenth and fourteenth centuries. And this, again, from the very beginning. Etienne Barbazan, in the preface to the first edition of the fabliaux (1756), claims, in a phrase later cited prominently by Brunetière, that the authors of the fabliaux were "excellens historiographes de la vie de chaque jour." For Le Grand d'Aussy, Barbazan's successor, "they show the nation undressed."[12] J. B. B. de Roquefort-Flaméricourt, writing on twelfth-century poetry before the rediscovery of La Chanson de Roland, concurs: "ce genre de poésie peignoit les actions ordinaires de la vie et les moeurs générales; c'est un miroir fidèle et véritable de l'Histoire civile et privée des François."[13]

De Roquefort-Flaméricourt's phrasing of the question of realism is not lost on de Montaiglon, who, again in the Introduction to the Recueil général, defines the fabliau as "un récit, plutôt comique . . . qui se passe dans les données de la vie humaine moyenne" (Recueil, I, vii).[14] At the outset, then, the fabliaux are perceived as the literary form of everyday life, the via regia to the ways supposedly "real people" worked, dressed, made themselves up, married, fornicated (position specific), slept, prayed, traveled, ate (menu specific), and drank in the High Middle Ages. Charles Langlois relies heavily upon them in La Vie en France au moyen âge as does Edmond Faral, who in La Vie quotidienne au temps de Saint Louis notes that "on les prendra pour de simples croquis d'après nature."[15]

So universally are the fabliaux assumed to contain the index of various medieval customs and castes that the "official" presentation of the genre by the Académie des Inscriptions et Belles-Lettres is organized according to the social condition of the chief protagonist of each tale. Victor LeClerc, editor of volume 23 of the *Histoire littéraire de la France* and a "membre de l'Institut," explains: "Pour nous acquitter du double soin de compléter les détails et d'apprécier l'ensemble, nous allons parcourir successivement, les fabliaux à la main, tous les rangs de la société."[16] "Fabliaux in hand," LeClerc looks right *through* them in order to present a hierarchical portrait of the saints, secular clergy, monks, knights and barons, bourgeois and peasants of the postfeudal era. Then too, a glance at the legion of German dissertations on the fabliaux shows the extent to which the easy assimilation of the comic tale to historical context had become, by the end of the nineteenth century, a virtual academic cottage industry: *Beiträge zur Kenntniss des altfranzösischen Volkslebens, meist auf Grund der Fabliaux*, P. Pfeiffer (1898); *Schilderung und Beurteilung der gesellschaftlichen Verhältnisse Frankreichs in der Fabliaudichtung*, F. Hermann (1900); *Die Frau in den altfranzösischen Schwänke*, A. Prieme (1901); *Der Vilain in der Schilderung der altfranzösischen Fabliaux*, W. Blankenburg (1902); *Liebe und Ehe in altfranzösischen Fablel und in der mittel hochdeutschen Novelle*, B. Barth (1910).[17]

The assumed transparency of the fabliaux has been summoned to prove just about anything and everything concerning the social reality of the High Middle Ages—another unsurprising projection given the enormous number and variety of tales involved.[18] Even the recent renaissance of medieval studies, which valorizes textual over historical concerns, has left the question of the comic tale's social realism virtually untouched. Indeed, beginning with the Annales School, refined methods of historical research continue to deepen our knowledge of the material conditions of medieval life and yet have led only to increasingly excessive claims concerning the mimetic accuracy of the fabliaux. Two recent books in particular herald a new and absurd plateau. Marie-Thérèse Lorcin, using ecclesiastical archives, concludes that the infrequent mention of sexual intercourse in what she delicately refers to as "la position 'rétro'" conforms to actual sexual practice; and by dipping into police files, she infers that "the corpus of the fabliaux offers a tableau of 'sexual transgression' thoroughly in keeping with what we find in contemporaneous judicial

records."[19] Similiarly, Philippe Ménard's reading of the fa-
bliaux, despite occasional words of caution, is literal to the ex-
treme. Ménard is certain, for example, that "when the author
of 'Le Vilain au buffet' tells us that the farmer had calloses on
his hands . . . he invents nothing"; or when we learn that the
miller's daughter in "Du Meunier et les deux clercs" sleeps in
an aerated trunk or bin (coffre), "this is not the burlesque in-
vention of our author. Such a custom really existed in certain
provinces, in certain families" (FM, pp. 53, 59). In comment-
ing on "Le Vilain Asnier," a tale in which a country cart driver
is overcome by the exotic smells of the city and revived when
a piece of excrement is placed under his nose, the erudite Sor-
bonne professor affirms that the carter is no amateur but a
"true specialist in the hauling of manure."[20] Ménard's obses-
sion with detail (and with excrement) leads him to corrobo-
rate in the *Manuel d'archéologie française* (Camille Enlart) the
monastic disposition of communal latrines in "Du Segretain
Moine" as well as the monks' preferred manner of wiping their
posterior parts: "On sait que des monastères avaient placé les
latrines au-dessus d'un cours d'eau. Nous découvrons qu'on
s'essuyait en ces lieux avec du foin" (FM, p. 57).

The fabliau's historical status as the literary form of social
history has, on the one hand, worked to deny the importance
of theory for their interpretation, while on the other hand, it
has (unwittingly?) contributed to the theory of the "natural
text."

The notion that one is able to read the fabliaux without any
critical apparatus is as old as our appreciation of the comic
tale. Bréal, for example, asserts that "l'interprétation est un
système trompeur, car il fait supposer que la fable est comme
un vêtement jeté sur la vérité pour laisser à l'esprit le mérite de
la découvrir. Les fables . . . ne contiennent aucun mystère;
elles ne sont ni des faits historiques déguisés, ni des allégories,
ni des métaphores, ni des symboles."[21] According to Jean
Rychner, medieval literature is in general "more engaged in
the social . . . less gratuitous, and less playful." In particular,
the fabliaux encourage "the avoidance of theoretical consid-
erations."[22] Ménard too claims that the thematic study of a
work of art needs no justification: "Quoique disent les écri-

vains, les situations parlent d'elles-mêmes. Elles ne trompent pas" (FM, p. 13).

Ménard's positing of "situations which speak for themselves" is in essence a version of the nineteenth-century notion of a natural work, born, as in G. Paris's account of the origin of the Indian fable, out of the "direct and ingenious observation of men of all social conditions."[23] Furthermore, such an articulation of textual production always works to undercut the specificity of the poetic object which—as a perfect mirror of the "simplicity and absence of affectation which still characterize the Orient" (G. Paris)—is itself without mystery, allegory, or metaphor, in short, without literary elaboration or manner. From the beginning the fabliaux have had the reputation of being without poetry. Joseph Bédier's slogan, according to which the medieval comic tale is "devoid of all literary pretention," indeed has become a commonplace of Old French studies.[24] Ferdinand Brunetière, for example, in reviewing Bédier's thesis for the *Revue des Deux Mondes*, accepts without question that the "literary value of the fabliaux, form or content, is nul."[25] Per Nykrog follows suit: "the genre of the light or humorous tale is, by definition, without literary artifice" (FN, p. 142).

What is interesting about the possibility of a literary text without literature is neither the esthetic nor the historical significance of such a critical posture, but that in this case the supposedly transparent work becomes the sign of poetic naturalism. Here again, the association of the frankness of the fabliaux with an original language predating the impropriety of metaphor is present from the beginning in Le Grand d'Aussy's Preface: "Soit simplicité du tems; soit qu'on crût qu'il n'y avait poit de mal, comme le dit le Roman de la Rose, à nommer ce que Dieu a fait; soit plutôt que la langue n'étant point formée, le libertinage n'eût pas encore inventé ces tours ingénieux, ces circonlocutions adroites qui parent la débauche en la voilant à demi; un chat chez les Fabliers est appellé un chat, & rien n'y est nommé que par son nom."[26] Or, in Bédier's articulation of the *locus classicus* of the simple, the naturel, and the true: "Ainsi—et tel est bien le caractère essentiel des fabliaux—le poète ne songe qu'à dire vitement et gaie-

ment son conte, sans prétention, ni recherche, ni vanité lit-
téraire. De là ces défauts: négligence de la versification et du
style, platitude, grossièreté. De là aussi des mérites, parfois
charmants: élégante [*sic*], brièveté, vérité, naturel" (FB,
p. 347). The fabliaux have offered historically the fantasy of a
language of beginnings, a poetic vehicle that remains to its ob-
ject invisible and therefore innocent, pristine, unencumbered
by artifice, unmannered and unrepressed—the transcription
of a "direct observation of men" in G. Paris's terms, a "sketch
from nature" in the phrase of Faral.

It is thus in the fabliaux that the deep medieval longing
for linguistic origins—the time before Babel—fulfills most
strongly the philological dream of discovering the original
roots of human language along with the romantic wish for the
"restoration of all things."[27] For if such a natural language is
thinkable, its very invisibility points to the simplicity of the
subject; and the imagined conformity of signifier to signified
engenders a romanticized world of innocence indistinguish-
able from that of imagined pleasures of the body. De Caylus
expresses such an alliance in his own feelings of loss with re-
spect to the world of the fabliaux: "on y connoissoit pleine-
ment la simplicité & la naïveté, qui seront toûjours la base
du goût vrai, & dont il semble qu'on s'écarte un peu trop
aujourd'hui" (*Mémoire*, p. 373). De Roquefort-Flaméricourt
equates simplicity of style with simple delights: "ce peuple,
naturellement joyeux, folâtre, léger et badin, inventa et perfec-
tionna le *Conte* ou *Fabliau* . . . . Ce poëme, de peu d'étendue,
ne consiste que dans une seule historiette, ordinairement gaie
et embellie par une manière de narrer simple et naïve" (*Etat*,
p. 188).

What I am suggesting is that the fabliaux constitute a limit
case of what has characterized to a lesser or greater degree the
discourse of medievalism for at least two centuries. As a privi-
leged ground of realism, the comic tale, more than any other
literary type, has fostered certain mystifications that are part
and parcel of what we have come to think of as the Middle
Ages.

The confusion of the "gay text" with that which it presents
is, first of all, responsible for the misperception of the era of

the fabliaux as a lost paradise, what Bédier refers to as "the happy epoch of the medieval period" (FB, p. 373). Second, the tenacious chimera of the transparent work has produced the ready association of a certain innocence of style with innocence of the flesh, a conflation of the body of representation and the body. The joy of storytelling becomes, in essence, that of the senses. Bédier again links "the same innocent and malicious joyousness, piquing lightly the surface of the skin" with "rapid sketches . . . jovial and light caricatures" (FB, p. 315). Lorcin confuses "crudity of vocabulary" with "uncomplicated sexuality" (*Façons*, p. 125). Ménard connects frankness of expression with "frank, simple, healthy sexuality and scatology" (FM, p. 162). Nykrog equates the comic tale's immunity from "literary artifice" with a "frank and naive pornography" (FN, p. 216). At an extreme, both historical and corporeal mystifications join. The innocent text permits direct access to the bodies and lives of poets as sociology and biography come together in an orgy of uncomplicated, simple delights. "Jean Bodel," writes Nykrog, "was, I believe, a likable man, without inner conflicts or deep hatreds; he was harmonious and happy, animated by a great and joyous love of life and of men. . . . Jean Bodel lived at a time when men were happy" (FN, p. 167).

A happy age, bodily naturalism, and the uninhibited, joyful "work without artifice" are, of course, synonymous with "l'esprit gaulois," that particular brand of nationalism attached to the Middle Ages and which even its detractors are anxious to acknowledge.[28] And if the scabrous tale is perceived to come always from elsewhere, it nonetheless somehow makes the French feel at home: "Secrétés par le pays de langue d'oïl, les fabliaux ne dépaysent pas leur public" (*Façons*, p. 7). From the beginning the French have made national claims upon the comic tale. Le Grand d'Aussy sees in them the first expression of a patrimonial genius continuous until the Classical Age:

> les Provinces qui aux douzieme & treizieme siecles produisirent les Romanciers & Fabliers français, sont celles-là mêmes qui au dix-septieme & au dix-huitieme ont

produit aussi Moliere, Boileau, Racine, Rameau, Cre-
billon, la Fontaine, Bossuet, Voltaire, Rousseau, Cor-
neille, Buffon, Condé, Turenne, le Brun, le Poussin,
Descartes, Vauban, &c. &c. &c.; c'est-à-dire, le génie,
l'éloquence, les belles imaginations, les talens sublimes,
les Poëtes fameux, & les grands Hommes enfin qui ont
illustré la France . . . (FA, p. lv)

De Caylus links such claims to what is perceived to be an in-
digenous capacity for bodily pleasure: "Je crois pouvoir avan-
cer que les François nés gais, légers & badins, ont saisi ce
genre de contes avec plus d'avidité que les autres nations d'Eu-
rope" (*Mémoire*, p. 356). De Caylus also speculates that France
would not in the past have needed to defend itself with arms
had it been armed with its "anciens manuscrits." [29] What is ar-
ticulated from the outset in terms of the natural—"the easy,
the clear, playfulness, a free and lively spirit" (FL, p. 79)—
comes to define the posterity of the fabliaux, which cannot be
detached from an implicit cultural hegemony. "& il me paroit
presque prouvé . . . qu'ils ont ensuite communiqué ce goût à
leurs voisins, sur-tout aux Italiens," continues De Caylus; "les
autres nations n'ont fait que les copier ou les imiter," echoes
Le Grand d'Aussy. [30] Even the antimedievalist, but pronation-
alist, Brunetière is quick to characterize their influence as
"cette première moisson du génie national." Chauvinism is
thus the defining principle of an almost ritual insistence upon
the fabliaux's importance for storytellers of other nations:
Boccaccio, Bandello, Sansovino, Straparole, Sacchetti, Ma-
lespini, Doni; Chaucer; Lope de Vega; the authors of the Ger-
man Schwänke and of the *Thousand and One Nights*.

How is it, then, that students of the fabliaux for over two
centuries have unrelentingly pursued the search for origins
and at the same time have maintained their affinity with some-
thing like the French national character? The answer lies, I
think, in the nature of what the French claim when they claim
the fabliaux and in the (not unlimited) strategies used to defend
against too great a consciousness of such an appropriation.

No one better than Brunetière understood the full impact
of what it means to embrace the obscene tale as one's own: "En

tant que satiriques, si 'Constant du Hamel' ou le fabliau du 'Prêtre qu'on porte' témoignent assez éloquemment de l'état d'âme de nos pères, leur attribuerons-nous cet autre mérite encore d'égaler, de remplir, d'épuiser la définition de 'l'esprit gaulois?' d'être vraiment caractéristiques d'une manière nationale de concevoir la vie? . . . dirons-nous des *Fabliaux* qu'ils expriment les traits essentiels du génie français? . . . il semble que les *Fabliaux* soient alors bien éloignés d'en être des modèles" ("Fabliaux," p. 197). In other words, to the extent that one insists upon the indigenous roots of the fable in the "regions of *langue d'oïl*," one is also forced to accept the scandal of the fabliaux—the excessiveness of their sexual and scatological obscenity, their anticlericalism, antifeminism, anticourtliness, the consistency with which they indulge the senses, whet the appetites (erotic, gastronomic, economic) and affirm what Bahktin identifies as the "celebration of lower body parts." Worse still, by laying claim to the fabliaux, the French, by their own admission, gain title to works which, according to classical esthetic criteria, are without literary value: "L'esprit gaulois est sans arrière-plan, sans profondeur, nous dit M. Bédier; il manque de métaphysique; il ne s'embarasse guère de poésie ni de couleur" ("Fabliaux," p. 197).

This suggests that the king's first question, the question of origins with which we began, is a direct response to his second query—"Who are you?"—and that it serves to defend the critic (and not only the Victorian critic) against the fundamental unacceptability of the fabliaux. Here again, Brunetière is aware of the paradox attached to seeing too much of oneself in the comic tale. In response to "whether or not they express the essential traits of French genius" he maintains: "C'est une question que l'on ne saurait résoudre sans avoir examiné celle de l'origine des *Fabliaux*" ("Fabliaux," p. 197). The antinaturalist, pronationalist critic deflects the unacceptability of the fabliaux toward the search for sources; he assumes that what is outrageous in them must come from somewhere else. "If, as we are told, *Tom Thumb* comes from India, why not the *Dit de la vieille Truande* as well?" ("Fabliaux," p. 197). Brunetière both makes and exposes the classical critical move— characteristic of almost all thinking about the fabliaux until

Bédier's clever shielding of the question of origins behind that of destination—which brings us back to the King of England and the Jongleur of Ely.

The king's third question—"Où vas tu?"—is a variation of the first two. It suggests the issue of audience which has monopolized the critic's attention ever since Bédier managed to diffuse the quest for origins with the concept of polygenesis and to reorient the question of beginnings toward that of intended public. Bédier himself begins from the premise that "the problem of origins is unsolvable and vain" (FB, p. 254). With a sharpness that, as we infer from the list on p. 5 above, discouraged no one, Bédier concludes that even where specific authors are concerned, "all our knowledge would not fill the inaugural dissertation of a single German student" (FB, p. 399). The fabliau originates nowhere, is everywhere, and at all times:

> Donc, où les contes populaires pour lesquels on édifie des théories sont-ils nés?
> Chacun d'eux en un lieu. Mais lequel? Nous ne le saurons jamais, puis qu'ils n'ont aucune raison d'être nés ici plutôt que là. . . .
> Quand ces contes sont-ils nés?
> Chacun d'eux un certain jour. Mais lequel? Nous ne le saurons jamais. (FB, p. 273–74)

Bédier's prediliction for autochthonous genesis thus preserves to a degree the honor of indigenous origin and cultural influence while defending against the horror of such a patrimony. If the French cannot take full credit for having invented the fabliaux, then no one can.

Bédier focuses upon the issue of audience as a compromise between the desire to appropriate an origin and the embarrassment of appropriation, between the temptation to project embarassment and the difficulty of renouncing that temptation. The notion of the spontaneously generated tale "each at a place . . . each at a time" serves as an antidote to the dangerous ambiguity of "l'esprit gaulois." Using the traditional equation of the level of literary discourse with intended public,[31] Bédier substitutes social difference for geographic and temporal difference. He establishes a totemic distance between the world of nobility, expressed in the epic and the romance, and that of the "little people" whose poetry (without poetry) is the fabliaux (*fabellae ignobilium*): "Il y a d'un bourgeois du XIIIe siècle à un baron précisément la même distance que d'un fabliau à une noble légende aventureuse" (FB, p. 371). In what sounds like the Gettysburg Address of medieval studies, Bédier asserts that "the fabliaux were born in the bourgeois class, by it, and for it" (FB, p. 20).

Bédier's view will, in turn, be countered by Per Nykrog who maintains that "the critic must refuse any distinction between publics, even within the upper echelons of society" (FN, p. 224). Nykrog replaces Bédier's affirmation of what amounts to liberal democracy in criticism with a critical oligarchy: ". . . il est impossible de séparer les fabliaux des milieux courtois. . . . Notre genre a trouvé son public principal dans ces cercles, il reflète les idées littéraires qui leur sont propres" (FN, p. 227). Finally, in what remains to date the most sophisticated treatment of audience, Rychner turns the rhetoric of Bédier's questions concerning time and place of origin on that of destination.[32] Rychner shows with consummate rigor that the style of even individual fabliaux varies. Through successive reworkings, which represent attempts to please diverse publics, the mobile medieval text is adapted either to bourgeois or to aristocratic taste: "Dans l'état du genre que présentent nos recueils, originaux, remaniements, et versions dégradées coexistent."[33] The subtlety of Rychner's demonstration still prevails. Thus Ménard: "Ni les jongleurs proches du peuple ni les lettrés n'ont le monopole des fabliaux" (FM, p. 96).[34]

Now what remains disturbing in even such a brief comparison of the king's three questions with those of the literary critic is not their similarity but the extent to which the fabliaux—of all the vernacular genres of the High Middle Ages—resist the defining issues of nineteenth-century philology. This may seem like a bold claim given the mass of work devoted to the discussion of source, theme or subject, and audience; yet it is sustained by even the most cursory reading of a textual corpus so elusive as to frustrate kings and scholars alike. To the question "Dont vien tu?" the jongleur replies "Je vienk de sà"; and when pressed ("Dont estez vus? ditez sanz gyle"), he continues:

> — Sire, je su de nostre vile.
> — Où est vostre vile, daunz Jogler?
> — Sire, entour le moster.
> — Où est le moster, bel amy?
> — Sire, en la vile de Ely.
> — Où est Ely qy siet?
> — Sire, sur l'ewe estiet.
> — Quei est le eve apelé, par amours?
> — L'em ne l'apele pas, eynz vint tousjours
> Volonters par son eyndegré,
> Que ja n'estovera estre apelée.
> — Tot ce savoi je bien avaunt.
> — Don qu demandez com enfant?
>
> *(Recueil, II, 243)*

— Sire, I am from our town. — Where is your town, Sir Jogler? — Sire, by the church. — Where is the church, good friend? — Sire, in the town of Ely. — Where is Ely? — Sire, it was on the water. — How is the water called by faith? — One doesn't call it; it always comes willingly of its own accord and never has needed to be called. — I knew all this before. — Then why did you ask like a child things you yourself already know?

To the question "Qy este vus?" the jongleur replies:

> — Sire, je su ou mon seignour.
> — Quy est toun seignour?" fet le Roy.
> "Le baroun ma dame, par ma foy.
> — Quy est ta dame par amour?
> — Sire, la femme mon seignour.
> — Coment estes vus apellee?
> — Sire, come cely qe m'ad levee.
> — Cesti qe te leva quel noun aveit?
> — Itel come je, sire, tot dreit.
>
> *(Recueil, II, 243)*

— Sire, I am the man of my lord. — Who is your lord?" asked the king. — "My lady's baron, by faith. — Who is your lady, please? — Sire, the wife of my lord. — What is your name? — Sire, the same as the one who raised me. — And that one, what name did he have? — The same as mine, sire, by right.

And, finally, to the question "Où vas tu?" the response is "Je vois de là."

These are but three of a series of a dozen or so parries that at every point in this Beckett-like encounter throw into question the king's authority—an authority attached to the possibility of naming properly and therefore of understanding positively, one that equates the question What is your name? with Whose man are you? Here, such influence is set against the power of poetry to refuse to specify its own origin, its destination, or even its own object. The positivity of the king's questions is in every instance turned back upon him:

> — Vendras tu ton roncyn à moy?
> — Sire, plus volenters que ne le dorroy.
> — Pur combien le vendras tu?
> — Pur taunt com il serra vendu.
> — Et pur combien le vendras?
> — Pur taunt come tu me dorras.
> — Et pur combien le averoi?
> — Pur taunt comme je recevroy.
> (Recueil, II, 244)

Will you sell me your horse? — Yes, more willingly than I would give it. — For how much will you sell it? — For as much as you will give me. — And for how much will I have it? — For as much as I shall receive.

Or, again:

> — De quele terre estez vus?
> — Sire, estez vus tywlers ou potters
> Qe si folement demaundez?
> Purquoi demandez de quele tere?
> Volez vus de moi potz fere?
> (Recueil, II, 247)

From what land are you? — Sire, are you a tiler or a potter who so foolishly asks from what land? Do you want to make a pot out of me?

"Le Roy d'Angleterre et le jongleur d'Ely" portrays a universe in which language seems to have lost purchase upon the world. In the place of answers the king—and the reader—encounters a series of slippages, tautologies, misunderstandings, substitutions, and complete disjunctions in which language—and poetic language in particular—is at every turn emptied of sense: "These words are nothing, says the king" ("Ces paroles . . . sunt neynz") to which the poet merely asks, "Of what use sense or knowledge? It's the same living in madness as in wisdom and courtesy" (Que val sen ou saver? / Ataunt valt vivre en folye / Come en sen ou corteysie" [*Recueil*, II, 249]).

On the surface this world upside down appears merely to belong to the rich tradition of medieval nonsense poetry—the *fatras*, *fatrasie*, *dervie*, *sotie*, and *farce*—and more specifically to the series of poems known as "La Riote del monde," of which the prose "Dit de l'herberie" (B.N., fr. 19152, f° 89) offers another example.[35] The poet's folly seems to anticipate the king's fool of Renaissance drama as well. After all, he reminds the king that "one often hears a fool speak sanely; and the wise man is the one who speaks wisely" ("Car um puet oyr sovent / Un fol parler sagement. / Sage est qe parle sagement" [II, 256]). Yet the jongleur's responses go much further. For he is aware that "sense" and "good sense" (*sen* and *saver*) are the conditions of the courtly or noble life and that madness or a lack of sense is—beyond any overtly radical social gesture—a condition of poetry, if not of all linguistic expression. Beneath his apparent foolishness lies a conscious meditation upon the rapport between the linguistic, the poetic, and the social, which, if evident in the king's equation of naming with control, becomes the subject of systematic speculation in the poet's discourse upon the inadequacy of all names and thus of all social categories.

In order to demonstrate the worthlessness of "sense" and "good sense," the jongleur of Ely undertakes to teach the king a lesson:

> Et tot vus mostroi par ensample
> Qu'est si large e si aunple
> E si pleyn de resoun,
> Que um ne dira si bien noun.

Si vus estez simple et sage houm,
Vus estez tenuz pour feloun;
Si vus parlez sovent e volenters,
Vus estes tenuz un janglers . . . (*Recueil*, II, 249)
E si vus les femmes amez,
E ou eux sovent parlez
E lowés ou honorez . . .
Donque dirra ascun pautener:
"Veiez cesti mavois holer,
Come il siet son mester
De son affere bien mostrer."
Si vus ne les volez regarder
Ne volenters ou eux parler,
Si averount mensounge trové
Que vus estes descoillé! . . . (II, 252)
Si je su mesgre: "Bels douz cher,
Mort est de faim; il n'a qe manger."
E, si je su gros e gras,
Si me dirra ascun en cas:
"Dieu! come cesti dorreit graunt flaut
En une longayne, s'il cheit de haut!"
Si j'ay long nees asque croku,
Tost dirrount: "C'est un bercu."
Si j'ay court nees tot en desus,
Um dirrat: "C'est un camus."
Si j'ay la barbe long pendaunt:
"Est cesti chevre ou pelrynaunt?"
E si je n'ay barbe: "Par seint Michel!
Cesti n'est mie matle, mès femmel."
E si je su long e graunt,
Je serroi apelé geaunt;
E si petitz sei de estat,
Serroi apelé naym e mat.
Dieu! come le siecle est maloré.
Que nul puet vivre sanz estre blamé!
(*Recueil*, II, 254)

And I will show you by examples that are so general and compelling and so full of reason that one cannot fail to agree. If you are a simple and wise man, you are taken for a rogue. If you speak often and willingly, you are taken for a loudmouth. . . . If you like women and speak often with them, frequent them, and praise and honor them . . . someone will say: "Look at that evil pimp who knows his work and shows it." If you refuse to look at them or to talk willingly with them, they will find the lie to prove that you are castrated. . . . If I am thin, they say: "Sweet little thing, you're dying of hunger; he doesn't have enough to eat." And if I am big and fat, there is always someone to say: "My God! what a big plop this one would make if he were to shit into a latrine, especially from high up." If I have a long crooked nose, they say: "He's a hooknose." And if I have a short stubby one, someone will say: "He's a pugnose." If I have a long beard hanging down, they ask: "Is this one a goat or a pilgrim?" And if I have no beard: "By Saint Michael! This one's no male but a woman." If I am big and tall, I am labeled a giant; but if I am small, I am labeled a dwarf and midget. My God! How the world is cursed when no one can live without blame!

The jongleur's speculation about the inappropriateness of names—all names—is of a piece with the king's deflected questions. Both cast doubt upon the adequacy of language ever to render even the simplicity of the body—nose or beard. "La Ruihote du monde" goes even further in its articulation of the incapacity of speech to be adequate even to itself:

> S'il se taist, il ne set parler;
> S'il parole, vés quel anpallier,
> Il ne cese onques de plaidier. . . .
> S'il cante bien c'est uns jongleres;
> S'il dist biaus dis, c'est uns trouveres.[36]

If a man is quiet, he is accused of not knowing how to speak; if he speaks, of being a loudmouth who never shuts up. . . . If he sings well, he is taken for a jongleur; and if he uses nice phrases, for a trouvère.

What the fabliaux—as speculation upon language as speculation—suggest, once again, is how strongly and explicitly the text resists the scholar's questions; and this refusal to specify an origin, a destination, or even to name itself throws into question the means by which the literary historian has sought up until now to understand—to name—the fabliaux.

How characteristic is "Le Roy d'Angleterre et le jongleur d'Ely"? It is one of a dozen or so tales that feature the poet as chief protagonist or that meditate specifically upon poetry. Further, I think that it can be shown that the fabliaux deal more directly than any other medieval genre not only with the conditions of the poet—his modes of living and production, his repertoire, his relations with patrons and with other poets, his social and economic status, his personal and family life— but with the art of poetry at the end of the Middle Ages. I would venture, moreover, that if the fabliaux have any coherence as a generic grouping (and the issue of "if" is worthy of serious consideration), this unity lies less in a single origin, thematics, intention, or form than in the sustained reflection upon literary language writ so large across these rhymed comic tales whose subject, mimetic realism notwithstanding, is the nature of poetry itself.[37] It is possible to read this enormous corpus (some 160 plus works) according to criteria that the poems themselves suggest. I am aware, of course, that often what passes for criticism when dealing with the fabliaux is a mere retelling of the plot as if their transparent common sense and a kind of self-evident humor might somehow speak for itself.[38] What I am suggesting, on the other hand, is another kind of inquiry, one that allows the text to address the issue it raises over and over again. That is: given that the jongleur can never adequately name himself, how does he go about naming that impossibility?

Such a strategy is not wholly foreign to existing treatments of the fabliaux. In fact, the reading proposed in the pages which follow is intimated sometimes in the margins, sometimes as the logical outcome, sometimes as a necessary negative deduction of some of the strongest discussions of the topic. It is obvious, for example, in Bédier's notions of the polygenesis of the fabliaux, since the universality of a spontaneous origin privileges implicitly the relation of the poet to poetic production. Bédier seems to be aware of this when, having exhausted the panoply of genetic explanations, he concludes that the only relevant question is "Quelles sont les conditions psychologiques universelles que suppose l'adoption universelle du conte?" (FB, p. 280).[39]

A specifically literary reading of the fabliaux is also obvious even in some of the more orthodox explanations of their origin. Indeed, to the extent that speculation about the comic tale tends to be radically genetic, it also tends to falter, to appear weak and fuzzy, to proffer obviously fictional and rhetorical explanations for that which remains unknown, to become in short, a parody of the very works whose source the critic seeks to capture. If, for example, Ten Brink's description of the fable's "long journey from India to the Atlantic ocean" is a masterpiece of imprecision, G. Paris's explanation of the frequent lack of resemblance between Old French versions and their source has all the earmarks of the series of fabliaux known as "De la longue nuit" or "Du Prêtre qu'on porte." Thus, in perfecting Benfey's reconstruction of the evolution of the *Pantchatantra*, Paris posits an original (lost) Sanskrit text translated into *pehlvi*, the language of Ancient Persia. From the (also lost) *pehlvi* text the tale produced a Syriac version which, Paris notes, "one once believed lost and even thought may have been imaginary, but which has been refound practically miraculously in an Armenian convent" (*Contes*, p. 13). The Syriac version produced an Arabic text; the Arabic, a Hebrew; the Hebrew, a Latin translation which was finally rendered into various vernacular tongues.

What is remarkable in this "official" story of how the *Pantchatantra* traveled from the banks of the Ganges to the Seine (5e arrondissement) is not so much the rigidity of the genetic linking, nor even the uncertainties attached to lost and possibly "imaginary" versions, but the fact that Paris also acknowledges the precariousness of each individual reworking and thus of each link in such a long textual chain:

> Souvent un premier intermédiaire a, pour des raisons indiquées, gravement déformé un conte: celui qui vient après, plus intelligent, plus réfléchi, s'aperçoit que les péripéties ne sont plus vraisemblables, que les actions des personnages ne sont plus motivées, que le conte ne répond plus au but que se propose celui qui le raconte;

alors il se met à l'oeuvre, supprime ce qu'il ne comprend pas, ajoute ce qui lui paraît nécessaire, répare plus ou moins bien, selon son imagination et son talent, les défauts qu'il a remarqués, et met alors le conte en circulation sous une forme qui ne ressemble plus que de bien loin à celle qu'il avait à l'origine. (*Contes orientaux*, p. 12).

It is hard to imagine a more explicit articulation of the fact that each link in the "long caravan of tales" is undermined by the vicissitudes of writing itself—the defects, dislocations, dispersions, "corrections," erasures, misperceptions and misplaced intentions, the imagined goals and hidden agendas of every individual poetic act. The route from the Ganges to the Seine is thus filled with detours that make every traveller on it the colleague of the jongleur of Ely, fellow disruptors of the coherence of origin, identity, and destination. All of which suggests as well that the essential relation in dealing with the fabliaux is that of the poet to language and not the hopelessly fragile link of a supposedly original (though often lost) source to a final version.

This brings us back to the epigraph with which we began, or to Brunetière's assertion that only if one denies the literary value of medieval literature can one begin to speak of it "and perhaps even to say interesting things about it." For Brunetière also has articulated what to date is perhaps the most interesting thing to be said about the fabliaux. That is, given the fragility of the process of transmission and the impossibility of ever recovering a definite origin, the ontologically founding power of words constitutes the most meaningful posture before the medieval comic tale:

Et, aussi bien, comme l'on dit que la fonction crée son organe, ne voyons-nous pas autour de nous, tous les jours encore, le mot—le Verbe—créer, lui aussi, son objet, le développer en quelque sorte, et l'organiser? ("Fabliaux," p. 205)

The essay which follows is in some extended sense the elaboration of the Word of which Brunetière speaks.

CHAPTER I

THE ILL-FITTING COAT
OF THE FABLIAUX

Et en aquesta maniera de dictar deu
hom far coma fan li teysshedor. qui
primieramen apparelho et ordissho los
fils. e pueysh teyssho lo drap.

Provençal Leys d'amors

(In this manner of composition one should do as the
weaver does, who first sets up the warp on his loom, and
then weaves the fabric.)

Deceite, wepyng, spynnyng hath yive
To wommen kyndely, whil that they may lyve.

CHAUCER

We begin with a tale less obviously concerned with poets and
poetry than "Le Roy d'Angleterre et le jongleur d'Ely," yet not
so different as it may seem. This is the tale of the ill-fitting coat,
"Du Mantel mautaillié," which stresses the fact that the fab-
liaux are all in some extended sense narratives of lack. Some-
one always wants something, whether sex, food, money, or as
in this case, a story itself. King Arthur, we are told, will not
sit down to dinner, "no matter how great the feast," without
first hearing a "tale of adventure."[1] The very word "adven-
ture" (from the Latin *ad+venire* and meaning "to happen," "to
happen by chance") is significant because it signals the spon-
taneous way in which the story is generated ("And it hap-
pened that a young knight appeared in the middle of the
road"), and because it is synonymous in fact with the tale we
read. There can be no distinction between the king's desire for
narrative and the fabliau which thus inscribes its own genesis.
Nor is it possible to distinguish the theme of "Du Mantel
mautaillié" from such a process, for the tale which "happens"
is in essence a story about the making of stories.

The knight who "arrives" or "happens along" carries an

adventure and a magic coat that will fit only the woman who has been faithful to her husband or lover:

> La fée fist el drap une oevre
> Qui les fausses dames descuevre;
> Ja feme qui l'ai afublé,
> Se ele a de rien meserré
> Vers son seignor, se ele l'a,
> Ja puis à droit ne li serra,
> Ne aus puceles autressi,
> Se ele vers son bon ami
> Avoit mespris en nul endroit
> Ja plus ne li serroit à droit
> Que ne soit trop lonc ou trop cort.
>
> (*Recueil*, III, 8)

The fairy who made it put the power to discover false ladies in the cloth. If the woman who puts it on has betrayed her husband in any way, it will never fit correctly. And the same is true for maidens who have wronged their lovers; the coat will never fit but will be either too long or too short.

As becomes painfully obvious in the course of more than one hundred public fittings in "Du Mantel mautaillié," the tailoring of the coat is assimilated to the tailoring of the tale. There is no means of separating the narrative economy of the fabliau from the economy of clothing. One right fit and the tale is too short; too many wrong fits and it never ends.

The identity between the garment that is slipped on (*afublé*) and the tale—the *flabel*—that is told (*afablé*) is striking. Further, the coat seems to embody a series of double truths that strike to the core of medieval thinking about such images. Not only does the garment which should cover work instead to discover or expose—as in the Celtic motif of the chastity-testing horn or mantle—but it constitutes an empty center of the story which it so strongly structures.[2] The coat cannot be represented, its representation being coterminous with the tale itself. There is, again, no distinction between the ill-fitting garment of fiction ("le mantel mautaillié") and that which lies beyond it, just as there is for the jongleur of Ely no way of cloaking the body—whether fat or thin, crooked- or pug-nosed—with an appropriate word.

The coat as representation and representation as a coat have a long history in the Middle Ages that is evident in both popular and learned traditions. The author of "La Vieille Truande," for example, assimilates fables or fabliaux to "cloth, shoes, socks, and songs":

> Des fables fet on les fabliaus
> Et des notes les sons noviaus,
> Et des materes les canchons,
> Et des draps, cauces et cauchons.
>
> (*Recueil*, V, 171)

Out of fables one makes fabliaux; out of notes, new sounds; out of material, songs; and out of cloth, socks and shoes.

Within the realm of high culture, Macrobius (fifth century) claims that:

> quia sciunt inimicam esse naturae apertam nudamque expositionem sui, quae sicut vulgaribus hominum sensibus intellectum sui vario rerum tegmine operimentoque subtraxit, ita a prudentibus arcana sua voluit per fabulosa tractari. sic ipsa mysteria figurarum cuniculis operiuntur ne vel haec adeptis nudam rerum talium natura se praebeat . . . . adeo semper ita se et sciri et coli numina maluerunt qualiter in vulgus antiquitas fabulata est, quae et imagines et simulacra formarum talium prorsus alienis, et aetates tam incrementi quam diminutionis ignaris, et amictus ornatusque varios corpus non habentibus adsignavit.[3]

> A frank and open exposition is distasteful to Nature, who, just as she has withheld an understanding of herself from the uncouth senses of man by enveloping herself in variegated garments, has also desired to have her secrets handled by more prudent individuals through fabulous narratives. Accordingly, her sacred rites are

veiled in mysterious representations so that she may not
have to show herself even to initiates. . . . In truth, di-
vinities have always preferred to be known and wor-
shipped in the fashion assigned to them by ancient
popular tradition, which made images of beings that had
no physical form, represented them as of different ages,
though they were subject neither to growth nor to decay,
and gave them clothes and ornaments, though they had
no bodies.

Thus, the relation of truth—Nature—to its representation or
image—to *narratio fabulosa*—is that of the body to clothes.

The magic coat of the Arthurian court is the robe of fable
and, more generally, a potent paradigm of representation in
Macrobius's terms—bodiless, empty, possessed only of ex-
terior signs, inadequate to cover the whole body, always too
short or too long. Both the late Latin pagan philosopher and
the anonymous author of the fabliau acknowledge literary
language (and indeed all language) to be insufficient, less ca-
pable of expressing a perceived reality exterior to it than of
covering up an absence, a lack of "physical form" which is es-
sentially scandalous. Macrobius continues:

Numenio denique inter philosophos occultorum curio-
siori offensam numinum, quod Eleusinia sacra interpre-
tando vulgaverit, somnia prodiderunt, viso sibi ipsas
Eleusinias deas habitu meretricio ante apertum lupanar
videre prostantes, admirantique et causas non conve-
nientis numinibus turpitudinis consulenti respondisse
iratas ab ipso se de adyto pudicitiae suae vi abstractas et
passim aduentibus prostitutas. (p. 8)

Numenius, a philosopher with a curiosity for occult
things, had revealed to him in a dream the outrage he
had committed against the Gods by proclaiming his in-
terpretation of the Eleusinian mysteries. The Eleusinian
Goddesses themselves, dressed in the garments of cour-
tesans, appeared to him standing before an open brothel,
and when in his astonishment he asked the reason for

this shocking conduct, they angrily replied that he had driven them from their sanctuary of modesty and prostituted them to every passer-by.

Beneath the garment of representation lies the disrepute of courtesans, just as beneath the ill-fitting coat of the Arthurian court lies the indiscretion of marital and courtly infidelity— even at the highest level:

> La Roine se porpensa
> S'ele fesoit d'ire samblant
> Tant seroit la honte plus grant;
> Chascune l'aura afublé;
> Si l'a en jenglois atorné.
>
> (*Recueil*, III, 12)

The queen thought to herself that if she made a pretense of anger the shame would only be greater; each one would have tried it on; she turned it into a joke.

The tale and the coat are linked in the assimilation of deceit— trickery, infidelity, lies, hiding—to poetic invention. Literary and sexual deception are equated; and if Arthur's desire for an "aventure" can be detached from his desire for the queen, the queen's desire to hide her adventures transforms her into a poet: "Si l'an en jenglois atorné."

Representation as a coat, the inadequation of the body and its garment, moral derogation inseparable from poetic deception—these are the elements of scandal writ large across the breadth of Old French literature. And this, again, from the beginning. Chrétien de Troyes, in what Claude Luttrell has termed "the first Arthurian romance," is obsessed by clothes and by the very association between dressing and writing found in Macrobius and in the "Arthurian fabliau":

> Li rois Artus sor l'un s'asist,
> sor l'autre Erec aseoir fist,
> qui fu vestuz d'un drap de moire.
> Lisant trovomes en l'estoire
> la description de la robe,
> si en trai a garant Macrobe

> qui en l'estoire a mis s'antante,
> qui l'antendié, que je ne mante.
> Macrobe m'aseigne a descrivre,
> si con je l'ai trové el livre,
> l'uevre del drap et le portret.
> Quatre fees l'avoient fet
> par grant san et par grant mestrie.[4]

King Arthur sat on one [throne]; Erec, who was dressed in a fine wool garment, sat on the other. Reading the story, we find the description of his robe. Macrobius, who applied his understanding to history and who understood it, offers proof that I am not lying. Macrobius taught me how to describe the craftsmanship and design of the cloth as I found it in the book. Four fairies made it full of meaning and art.

Inspired by "Macrobius's book," the "portraits" on Erec's robe, or the arts of the *quadrivium*, constitute a microcosm of the physical world—a *speculum mundi* whose designs and detail supposedly exhaust the possibilities of representation. Geometry encompasses the measure "from top to bottom" of the globe; Arithmetic, the number of "drops in the sea . . . and stars in the sky"; Music, the "harmony of instruments and of song"; and Astronomy, a "vision of what was and shall be" (*Erec*, vv. 6684–6747).

Erec's cosmic coat is merely one of a series of garments which figure prominently in Chrétien's romance. In fact, this last robe, which is synonymous with the hero's telling of his own tale of adventure (*Erec*, vv. 6414–6446), attests to the impossibility of further narrative progression, just as Enide's dress in the beginning signals the necessity of quest:

> La dame s'an est hors issue
> et sa fille, qui fu vestue
> d'une chemise par panz lee,
> delïee, blanche et ridee;
> un blanc cheinse ot vestu desus,
> n'avoit robe ne mains ne plus,
> et tant estoit li chainses viez

que as costez estoit perciez:
povre estoit la robe dehors,
mes desoz estoit biax li cors.

    Molt estoit la pucele gente,
car tote i ot mise s'antante
Nature qui fete l'avoit.

(Erec, v. 401)

The lady came out with her daughter, who was dressed
in a shift with wide panels which were unlaced, white,
and wrinkled; she wore a white blouse, but had no other
garment; and the blouse was so old that it was ripped on
the sides. The dress was poor on the outside, yet the
body beneath it was beautiful.

    The maiden was very comely, for Nature, who had
made her, had given herself wholly to it.

To the extent that Erec's robe contains a plenitude of natural
phenomena, it signifies properly the fullness of Nature, a cer-
tain semiological adequation, and narrative closure. The dif-
ference or gap between Enide's body and her dress, on the
other hand, circumscribes a distance between Nature and its
representation that is the equivalent of a lack of linguistic
property.[5]

Enide's old and tattered blouse stands as the improper des-
ignation of her true inner worth, an impropriety that is syn-
onymous with the economic condition of the family who
cannot afford to clothe her. Enide's father says to his future
son-in-law:

Biax amis, fet li vavasors,
povretez fet mal as plusors
et autresi fet ele moi.
Molt me poise, quant ge la voi
atornee si povrement,
ne n'ai pooir que je l'amant:
tant ai esté toz forz an guerre,
tote en ai perdue ma terre,
et angagiee, et vandue.

(Erec, v. 509)

> Good friend, said the vavasor, poverty does ill to many
> as it has done to me. It pains me greatly, when I see her
> dressed so poorly, and I don't have the means to do any-
> thing about it. I have waged war so long that I have lost,
> mortgaged, and sold all my lands.

The loss of ancestral property ("tote en ai perdu ma terre")
and the lack of a proper dress ("ge la voi / atornee si povre-
ment") are the signs of a double divestiture which Erec prom-
ises to redress.[6]

The first part of Chrétien's romance—"li premier vers"—
is about the attempt to clothe Enide; and the bestowal of a
proper dress (the "best of which Nature is capable") remains
inseparable from the reinvestiture of her parents (*Erec*, vv.
1835–1838) as well as the imposition of a proper name.[7] Nor
can the semantic nexus of proper dress and linguistic and eco-
nomic property be disentangled from poetry itself. The "Joy
of the Court," with which the romance ends, is present in
germ from the beginning and transforms the marital celebra-
tion into a celebration of verse:

> Quant la corz fu tote asanblee,
> n'ot menestrel an la contree
> qui rien seüst de nul deduit,
> qui a la cort ne fussent tuit.
> An la sale molt grant joie ot.
>
> (*Erec*, v. 1983)

> When the court was gathered, there was not a minstrel in
> all the land who knew anything about entertainment
> who was not at court. Inside there was great joy.

Robing, naming, and the restoration of ancestral property are,
on the level of theme, sufficient causes of a poetic celebration
which serves to inscribe Chrétien within the romance attached
to his own name. And that inscription, the sign of the poet's
presence before the Other (if only the Otherness of writing)
is, in turn, intended to elicit the robing of the poet:

> Ce jor furent jugleor lié,
> car tuit furent a gré paié:

> tot fu randu quanqu'il acrurent,
> et molt bel don doné lor furent:
> robes de veir et d'erminetes,
> de conins et de violetes,
> d'escarlate, grise ou de soie;
> qui vost cheval, qui volt monoie,
> chascuns ot don a son voloir
> si boen com il le dut avoir.
>
> (*Erec*, v. 2055)

That day jongleurs were happy, for all were paid to satisfaction. To all was rendered what was due, and many a beautiful gift was distributed: coats of fur and ermine, of rabbit, and of purple and crimson, of common cloth or of silk. One wanted a horse, another money. Each had a gift according to his wish and as good as he deserved.

Erec et Enide oscillates between the initial inadequacy of the dress of the heroine and the plenitude of the robe of the hero. The attempt to redress what is sensed as a gap between the body and its representation defines the parameter of a search for meaning (or property) that is ontologically prior even to the theme of chivalric quest. The *seriatim* capture of thieves involved in Erec's recuperation of his knightly worth is, in other words, the external manifestation of a more central ordeal. This test, the repeated prohibition of speech and the breaking of silence, is that of the poet himself. Chrétien's implicit request for rewards in the fancy gowns bestowed upon jongleurs makes him, then, simultaneously a rober and a robber.

The association of poetry and clothes is present from the beginning of the Old French lyric. Indeed, the earliest examples, known as the *chanson d'histoire* or the *chanson de toile*, are supposedly the products of the woman's weaving room, and they make even clearer the connection we have traced thus far. Not only does the singer often sit embroidering ("Bele Erembours a la fenestre au jor / sor ses genolz tient paile de color"), but the poem we read becomes virtually indistinguishable from the embroidered garment:[8]

> Bele Yoland en ses chambres seoit.
> D'une boen samiz une robe coloit:
> a son ami tramettre la voloit.
> En sospirant ceste chançon chantoit: . . .
> Bels douz amis, or vos voil envoier
> une robe par mout grant amistié.[9]

Beautiful Yolanz was sitting in her chambers. She was sewing a good robe of samite to send to her true love. Sighing, she was singing this song: . . . Good sweet love, now I want to send you a robe out of such great feeling.

Sewing and singing go hand-in-hand, as the garment of representation seems in "Bele Yolanz" to summon, or even to produce, the lover: "A ces paroles et a ceste raison, / li sieus amis entra en la maison."[10]

Poems about the making of poems, the *chansons de toile* afford a privileged glimpse of the conditions surrounding poetic performance in the High Middle Ages. We know this from Jean Renart's *Guillaume de Dole*, which makes explicit the connection between poetic voice, desire, and text and which furnishes contemporaneous commentary upon the mode of production of the weaving song. Guillaume, showing the messenger the women's workroom, brags of his mother's millinary and musical skills.[11] She, in turn, obliges with an explanation of the place of singing—and a song:

> "Biaus filz, ce fu ça en arriers
> que les dames et les roïnes
> soloient fere lor cortines
> et chanter les chançons d'istoire! . . ."
> Lors commença seri et cler:
> Fille et la mere se sieent a l'orfrois,
> a un fil d'or i font orïeuls croiz.
> Parla la mere qui le cuer ot cortois.
> Tant bon'amor fist bele Aude en Doon!
>
> "Aprenez, fille, a coudre et a filer,
> et en l'orfrois orïex crois lever.

L'amor Doon vos covient oublier."
Tant bon'amor fist bele Aude en Doon.

(Guillaume de Dole, vv. 1148, 1158)

"Dear son, it was back here that ladies and queens used
to make their drapes and sing *chansons d'histoire!* . . ."
Then she began pleasantly and clearly: Daughter and
mother sit trimming. With golden thread they embroi-
der crosses of gold. The mother speaks with a noble
heart. Oh the sweet love of Aude in Doon!

"Learn, my daughter, to knit and sew, and place gold
crosses in the trim. You must forget Doon's love." Oh
the sweet love of Aude in Doon!

Like the decoration of the robe Guillaume's mother sews, the
lyric insert decorates narrative. More important, her song re-
produces the external situation of mother and daughter in the
workroom at the time of Guillaume's boast. The relation of
gesture and voice thus seems reversed as the mother contained
in "Fille et la mere se sieent a l'orfrois" teaches the daughter of
the narrative, Guillaume's sister Lïenor, how to sing another
chanson d'histoire: "Siet soi bele Aye as piez sa male maistre."[12]
The narrative which frames the lyric inserts of *Guillaume de
Dole* are similar to the *razos* of the troubadours, the expla-
nations or "causes" surrounding the Provençal *vers*.[13] In the
razos, however, the imbrication of commentary and praxis is
not nearly so complete as in this representation of the weav-
ing of a song about the weaving of songs. A seamless web in
which it is impossible to separate telling from singing, com-
ing into being from being, the *chanson de toile* seems, as much
as it is possible, to be made of whole cloth.

The coat as representation and representation as a coat are
also evident in contemporaneous allegorical works both in
Latin and in the vernacular. Nature's robe in Alain de Lille's *De
Planctu Naturae*, for example, serves, like Erec's robe, as a mir-
ror of the physical world: "Vestis autem ex serica lana con-
texta, multifario protecta colore, puellae pelli serviebat in
usum" (*De Planctu*, col. 435).[14] Alain's imagery will be ap-
propriated by Guillaume de Lorris for whom the scandal of

Nature's garment becomes the equivalent of an entire literary mode. Within the *Roman de la Rose*, the breaking of the poet's silence and the awakening of sexual desire are explicitly bound to the cloaking of Nature's body:

> Lors devient la terre si gobe,
> Que veut avoir novele robe;
> Si fait si cointe robe faire
> Que de colors y a cent paire
> D'erbes, de flors indes et perses
> Et de maintes colors divers.[15]

Then the earth became so vain (engorged) that she wanted a new dress; it had such a beautiful dress made that there are a hundred pairs of colors of herbs and flowers of violet and blue and of many different colors.

Each allegorical image is constructed around the principle of dress: Avarice wears "an old coat"; Sadness, "a torn coat"; and Poverty, no coat at all.[16] Guillaume is aware, moreover, that allegory functions according to the representation of isolated essences (natures) of things and that the atomization of the allegorical image renders it partial and defective. The robe of Nature is always in pieces. Thus the repeated play upon the verb "deviser" meaning both "to describe" and "to divide." The allegorist is, at bottom, a cutter of cloth: "C'est la robe que je devise" (*Rose*, v. 65); "Mes de sa robe devisier / Criens durement qu'entrepris soie. . . ." (*Rose*, v. 876). The cuts or divisions inflicted upon Nature's supposedly naked body are, as Guillaume suggests, none other than the distance that language inscribes between the object and its poetic representation, a displacement synonymous with the etymological definition of allegory as "to mean otherwise."

For Jean de Meun the dismemberment of the body is associated with representation as cutting or, to be more specific, with the question of how to name that which Saturn lost at the time of his castration.[17] Corporeal mutilation is, in other words, the proper sign of the impropriety of all signs. The robing of the mutilated body, as Faux-Semblant makes clear, comes to stand for the scandal of imitation:

Je sai bien mon habit changier,
Prendre l'un et l'autre estrangier.
Or sui chevalier, or sui moine,
Or sui prelat, or sui chanoine,
Or sui clerc et or sui prestre,
Or sui desciple et or sui mestre,
Or chastelain, or forestiers,
Briement, je sui de touz mestiers.
Or sui princes et or sui pages,
Or sai parler tretouz languages.

(*Rose*, v. 11187)

I know how to change my clothes, put on one set and take off the other. Now I am a knight, now a monk, now a prelate, now a canon, now a clerc; now I am a priest, now a disciple, now a master, now a castellan, now a woodsman. In short, I am a jack-of-all-trades. Now I am a prince, now a page; for I know how to speak all languages.

Ultimately, the disreputableness of poetry lies in the mobility of its signs—the prince who is a page and, indeed, the page that we read; the page that "knows how to speak all languages." Every semblance is, according to the above inscription of the poet as a "quick-change artist," a Faux-Semblant.

This suggests that the fabliaux with which we began, and which seemed at first so idiosyncratic, are the products neither of madness nor of reaction against other supposedly more coherent generic types; they contain neither folly nor the makings of a countergenre.[18] On the contrary, "Le Roy d'Angleterre et le jongleur d'Ely" and "Du Mantel mautaillié" are indicative of a way of thinking about representation that is characteristic of a variety of forms as different from them (and each other) as the allegory, lyric, and romance.[19] These tales merely make explicit what is less focused elsewhere—the importance of the metaphoric equation of language and clothing, the insufficiency of both to cover what is conceived (as presence) to be the naked body of Nature, and the inherent scandal associated with the cover-up of such a failure.

The "riotous fable" and the "textile text" serve to uncover

the opprobrium attached to poetry; such an uncovering forces a revision of the ways we traditionally have sought to understand Old French literature—the fabliaux in particular. It means that the scandal of the comic tale is not that which traditionally is associated with "l'esprit gaulois." Their disreputableness is not that they contain dirty words, celebrate the body in all its concavities and protrusions, revel in scatology, or even that they poke fun at villainous aristocrats, lecherous priests, and insatiable women, but that they expose so insistently the scandal of their own production. They explicitly reveal not so much a moral as a poetic derogation—poetry as derogation. In this "Le Roy d'Angleterre et le jongleur d'Ely" and "Du Mantel mautaillié" merely hint at the multiple modes of disruption by which the authors of the fabliaux conceive of their own undertaking.

Poetry is, first of all, theft—a matter not only of garments which cover and cover up, but of lost coats. Thus the priest of "Estula," responding to the peasant's plea for help, takes up his mantle—"Li prestres a prise l'estole"—only to leave it on a farmyard post: "Mès son soupeliz ahocha / A .I. pel, si qu'il remest là" (*Recueil*, IV, 90). Gathered by thieves who menace the priest with dismemberment, the stolen stole serves to structure the comic tale and to define its specific literary effects. For the garment left in the place of a lost member transforms the thieves' despair into joy:

> Lors a cil moustré son conquest,
> Qu'ot gaaignié le soupelis;
> Si ont assez gabé et ris,
> Que li rires lor fu renduz,
> Qui devant lor fu desfenduz.
>
> (*Recueil*, IV, 91)

Then he showed his gain, the one who had captured the mantle; they joked and laughed quite a bit, since laughter was restored to them, it having been prohibited before.

Similarly, the tale, itself a supplement to dismemberment, restores, as its moral infers, the joy of the beholder: "Tel rit au main qui au soir pleure, / Et tels est au soir corouciez / Qui au mains est joianz et liez."[20]

The association of the stolen stole and the displaced letter is general within the fabliaux, which repeatedly equate the pilfering of cloth with linguistic ruse. "Dieus! ma toille, je l'ai perdue" (*Recueil*, IV, 151), exclaims the desolate draper Brifaut, whose wife, like the thieves of "Estula," transforms his name into a common noun: "Si com tu as mençonge dite! . . . Brifaut, vous l'avez brifaudée" (*Recueil*, IV, 152). Brifaut is a "Pathelin avant la lettre," one whose loss becomes a by-word for the particular scandal of gluttony.[21]

The connection between divestiture and deception is a virtual leitmotif. The lecherous priest of "Le Dit dou Soucretain," for example, offers to divest himself of his possessions in return for sexual favors—"Vous averez joiaus et roubes"— to which the burger's suspicious wife replies: "ce sont bien lobes" (*Recueil*, VI, 118). Over and over again the word "robes" is rhymed with "lobes," or lies, as robing, robbery, and poetry are, from the beginning, aligned. Richeut, the heroine of what is generally considered the earliest fabliau, is more effective by her tricks than those who steal outright: "Plus conquiert el par sa boidie / Et par sa lobe / Que cil qui prant et tost et robe."[22] The clever prostitute convinces each of her clients that he has impregnated her ("N'i a celui cui el ne die / Que de lui est ele enpraingnie" ["Richeut," v. 383]), as her son Sanson, who even *in utero* is the vehicle of deception, grows up to be the master of ruse:

> Moines devint a Clervax,
> S'ot les blans dras, s'ert moines faux . . .
> Si en porta tot lor tresor. . . .
> Jusq'au flun Jordain n'a maison
> Ne covant de relegion
> O n'ait pris ordre. . . .
> Trestoz les robe,
> Pechié ne dote ne oprobre,
> Toz les vaint Sansons par sa lobe. . . .
> Mar lo crïerent les nonains,
> Car les plusor en fist putains

> Puis les roba. . . .
> Une abeesse
> En amena grosse et espesse,
> Puis devint ele jugleresse.
>
> ("Richeut," v. 895)

He became a monk at Clervaux; but even though he took the white cloth, he was a false monk. . . . He carried away their treasure. . . . From here to the river Jordan there was not a house or convent whose order he did not embrace. . . . He robbed them all; nor did he fear sin but conquered them all with his ruse. . . . To their dismay many nuns believed him, for he turned many to prostitution and then robbed them. . . . One abbess whom he left good and pregnant later became an entertainer.

Sanson's robbing depends on his robing. And if he transforms his victim into a performer ("Puis devint ele jugleresse"), it is because he incarnates the polyvalent possibilities of false seeming identified with poetry itself.

Jean de Meun—through the figure of Faux Semblant—equates the changing of garments with a certain mobility of social identity and with poetic invention. So too, Sanson, the offspring of so many fathers that paternity becomes just another fiction, is simultaneously rober ("S'ot les blans dras"), robber ("Trestoz les robe"), and poet. The author of "Richeut" goes out of his way to praise Sanson's precocious gift for letters, grammar, and for song.[23] All of which makes his capacity for dressing, lying, and stealing part and parcel of the greatest ruse of all: "Plus set Sanson / Rotruange, conduiz et sons; / Bien set faire les lais bretons" ("Richeut," v. 798).

The identification of poetry, clothes, and theft is perhaps most evident in "De Barat et de Haimet." Even the names of two of the felons connote crookedness (Travers) and ruse (Barat), as the three thieves literally "steal the pants" off each other. To Barat's jibe of being without trousers Haimet replies with a thievish boast—"Si ai, fet il, trestoutes nueves, / Dont j'emblai l'autre jor la toile"—only to discover them gone:

Haimès soulieve ses girons:
De ses braies nules ne vit,
Aing vit ses coilles et son vit
Trestout descouvert nu à nu.

(Recueil, IV, 96)

Haimès lifts his apron; his pants were not visible. All you could see were his balls and prick all exposed and naked.

Travers's admiring comment that "Barat is a thieves' thief" ("Bien est lerres qui larron emble") places specifically verbal ruse at the top of the trickster's scale ("N'a tel larron jusqu'a Nevers / Comme est Baras. . . ."). Barat's wife, however, makes the connection of such ruse to poetry even more explicit. Her greeting upon the thief's return—"'Sire, bien soiez vous trovez'" (*Recueil*, IV, 108)—can be read to mean both "welcome home" and "how well you are crafted." The product (as well as the essence) of the trouvère's ruse, Barat is indeed "bien trovez."

Like Sanson and Barat, the poet comes from a line of thieves—specialists in the taking of coats. One jongleur says to another in the tale known as "La Contregengle":

Qui fu ton pere et qui ta mere?
Je les conui bien, par Saint Pere:
Tes peres embla .I. tabar
Par qoi il fu penduz à Bar,
Et en meïsme cele anée
Fu ta mer à Provins plantée;
Je vi une teue seror
Qui espousa .I. lecheor;
Andui furent planté ensamble
A Miaus le Chastal, ce me samble;
Por .I. sorcot qu'ele ot emblé
Furent ensamble andui planté.

(Recueil, II, 260)

Who was your father and your mother? I knew them well by the Holy Father: your father stole an overcoat for which he was hanged that same year at Provins. I saw your sister marry a lecher; both were hanged together at Maius le Chastal, it seems to me, for an overcoat she had stolen.

Here the connection between stolen clothes and a corrupt genealogy underscores the extent to which the fabliau obscures its own suspicious origins, the extent to which all such tales partake of a perpetual illegitimacy. The jongleur continues:

> Estrais est de pute lingnie
> Je revie ja de ta mesnie
> Lez moi que j'avoie à voisins
> .II. maus larrons de tes cousins;
> Andui furent par bougresie
> Ars en milieu de Normandie.
>
> (*Recueil*, II, 260)

You come from a stinking line. Not long ago I saw your family who used to live beside me, including these two evil thieving cousins of yours; both were burned for sodomy in the middle of Normandy.

The robe of representation is not only to some degree or other always displaced, but is turned away, subverted, or perverted.

The association of poetry, robbery, ruse, and fornication is a common one. Indeed, the author of the tale known as "Du Fotéor" makes no distinction between the status of the protagonist as trickster and poet ("Menestrex sui" [*Recueil*, I, 305]) and his role as a professional fornicator:

> Ge sui fouterres à loier. . . .
> La laide me done sols .C.
> Par ce que ele l'aise sent,
> Et la bele me done mains.
>
> (*Recueil*, I, 310–11)

I am a fornicator for rent. . . . The ugly woman gives me 100 sous to feel good, and the beautiful one gives me less.

What I am suggesting, however, is that this nexus of ideas also involves the mutual implication of theft, poetry, and perver-

sion. The alienation of property implies verbal disappropria-
tion, alienation of the proper; this deflection of both an eco-
nomic and linguistic order carries with it sexual infraction as
well:[24]

> Tu paroles moult folement.
> Si me fex si .I. argument
> Et .I. sofisme tout boçu.
> Mes, chetis houliers, qui es tu? . . .
> Tu n'as pas ta borde vendue,
> Qui ainsi bestornes les nons.
> Tu es li sages Salemons,
> Qui tant aprist que en folie
> Torna le sens de sa clergie.
> Tant as vescu que tu radotes,
> Et t'avis que, pour .II. cotes
> Que tu as environ tes os
> Que nus ne soit jamès si os
> Que il devant toi parler ost. . . .
>
> (*Recueil*, II, 257–58)

You speak foolishly and construct for me a hunchbacked
argument; but, unfortunate pimp, who are you any-
way? . . . You have not sold your tricks, you who per-
vert names. You are like the wise Solomon who learned
so much he turned his wisdom into folly. You've lived so
long you talk nonsense, and you think because of the
two coats you are wearing that no one would dare to
challenge you.

Poetry is sophistry, trickery, pimping, madness, and prostitu-
tion; and it is perceived as an act against nature.

Here is where a vernacular poetics joins the Latin tradition.
For the connection made in "La Contregengle" between the
wearing of two coats, sophistry, and sodomy is best expressed
in the *De Planctu Naturae*. According to Alain, Nature's robe,
the inventory of all living things, is always double or du-
plicitous because it obscures the difference between oppo-
sites—between the self and others, between fiction and its
Other. Youth is transformed into old age: "Illic aquila post
juvenam secundo senem induens, iterum in Adonidem re-

vertebatur a Nestore"; death into life: "Illic phoenix in se mortuus, redivivus in alio, quodam naturae miraculo, se sua morte a mortuis suscitabat" (*De Planctu*, col. 435).[25] Species are crossbred, exchange offspring, and even metamorphized into one another. But, most of all, the robe is confused with that which it supposedly represents. The marten and sable images in Nature's robe become interwoven with the mantle itself: "Illic martes et sabelo, semiplenam palliorum pulchritudinem eorum postulantem subsidia, suarum nobilitate pellium, ad plenum deducebant" (*De Planctu*, col. 438).[26]

Representation, for Alain de Lille, exudes the odor of scandal attached to a smearing of the distinction between the body and its image: "Haec animalia, quamvis illic allegorice viverent, ibi tamen esse videbantur ad litteram" (*De Planctu*, col. 436).[27] And if the figures on Nature's robe are essentially unnatural, it is because they obscure the ultimate difference between life and death; they make mute Nature speak: "Illic psittacus, cum sui gutturis incude, voci monetam fabricabat humanae. Illic coturnicem figurae draconis ignorantem fallaciam, imaginariae vocis decipiebant sophismata" (*De Planctu*, col. 436).[28] The *De Planctu Naturae* is a treatise on the relationship between poetry and perversion. For Nature, whose role it is to guarantee the "lawful path of sure descent," has as her handmaiden two instruments of rectitude—*ortho*graphy, or straight writing, and *ortho*dox coition, or straight sexuality. She is, however, at every turn literally turned away from the straightness of grammar by rhetoric which is the equivalent of sexual deviance:

> Sicut autem quasdam grammaticae dialecticaeque observantias inimicantissimae hospitalitatis incursu volui a Veneris anathematizare gymnasiis; sic metonymicas rhetorum propositiones, quas in suae amplitudinis gremio rhetorica mater amplectens, multis suas rationes conflat honoribus, Cypridis artificii interdixi, ne si nimis durae translationis excursu a suo reclamante subjecto, praemium alienet in aliud, in facinus facetia, in rusticitatem urbanitas, tropus in vitium in decolorationem color nimius convertatur. (*De Planctu*, col. 458)

Just as I decided to excommunicate from the schools of
Venus certain practices of Grammar and Dialectic as in-
roads of the most ill-disposed enemy, so too I banned
from the Cyprian's workshop the use of words by the
rhetors in metonymy which Mother Rhetoric clasps to
her ample bosom and breathes great beauty on her ora-
tions, lest, if she embark on too harsh a trope and trans-
fer the predicate from its loudly protesting subject to
something else, cleverness would turn into a blemish,
refinement into boorishness, a figure of speech into a de-
fect and excessive embellishment into vice. (De Planctu,
p. 162)

The association of sophistry—linguistic artifice, excessive or-
nament, show—and sodomy lies at the core of Alain's own
tricky thought. Those who "push the laws of grammar too
far" and defy Nature's rule of straightness find themselves, as
in Dante's placement of Brunetto Latini, among the sodom-
ites. The poet belongs to the line of Jocus, those who em-
brace—through simulacrum—the art of *gai saber*.

The identification of poetry and perversion is evident in a
broad range of vernacular forms and points to the imbrication
of medieval poetics and practice. Thus Gautier de Coinci's
"Seinte Léocade," which was published in the Méon/Bar-
bazan edition of the fabliaux, defines bestiality as an essen-
tially grammatical sin equivalent to an erasure of lineage from
the Book of Nature:

> Il metent hic en totes parz;
> La gramaire hic à hic acouple,
> Mais nature maldit la couple.
> La mort perpetuel engenre
> Cil qui aimme masculin genre
> Plus que feminin ne face,
> Et Diex de son livre l'efface. . . .[29]

They put *hic* everywhere; grammar couples *hic* with *hic*,
but nature curses such a couple. The one who loves the
masculine gender more than the feminine engenders
perpetual death, and God erases him from His Book.

Despite his own warning, the poet is the one who joins like to like, or obscures meaning through the surface play of phonetic resemblance: "Tout ont noié jusqu'à Noion, / Se toz en Oyse nes noion, / Touz ert, ce cuit, ainz quatre mois / Noions noiez et Noiemois / Noions les toz, noions, noions, / Ainz que noiez en soit Noions"; or, "Nostre Dame est Dame des Dames, / Dame est des cors et Dame d'ames" (*Fabliaux et contes*, vv. 1537, 2159).

What is at stake in the loss of phonetic difference is a loss of sexual determinacy, a loss Alain again equates with the heteroclitic (and essentially dangerous) nature of poetry:

> Eorum siquidem hominum qui Veneris profitentur grammaticam, alii solummodo masculinum, alii feminum, alii commune, sive promiscuum genus familiariter amplexantur: quidam vero heterocliti genere, per hiemem in femino, per aestatem in masculino genere irregulariter declinantur. (*De Planctu*, col. 450)

> Of those men who subscribe to Venus' procedures in grammar, some closely embrace those of masculine gender only, others those of feminine gender, others, those of common or epicene gender. Some, indeed, as though belonging to the heteroclite class, show variations in deviation by reclining with those of female gender in winter and those of masculine gender in summer. (De Planctu, p. 136).

It is, ultimately, the mobility of poetic and sexual identity that represents for Nature the most potent threat to the *straight*ness—*correct*ness, *regular*ity, *ortho*doxy—of grammar, which, from the Greek *gramma*, means line. Against Nature, the poet is the one who, according to the troubadour Bernart Marti, "will transform a bitch into a sire and raise today until tomorrow."[30]

The displaced robe of representation is the sign of an always implicit transvestism. As we have seen, the jongleur as trickster in "De Barat" "steals the pants" off his companion; and such an act is associated with the ruses of poetry. In "Des Braies au cordelier" an unwitting exchange of pants is linked explicitly to writing. Thus the unsuspecting husband, having picked up his wife's lover's trousers instead of his own ("Quar li sires a si mespris / Que les braies au clerc a pris" [*Recueil*, III, 281]), discovers in his pocket the instruments of orthography instead of his purse: "Si a trové une escritoire, / Où li canivez au clerc ere, / Et son parchemin, et sa penne" (III, 284). The poet plays on the words *trover*, meaning both "to find" and "to invent" in the sense of poetic invention, and *borse*, meaning both "money pouch" and "testicles." The cuckold, dressed like the poet in the clothes of another, discovers through the tools of writing that he has been castrated: "Par poi li borgois ne forsenne, / Quant il sa borse n'a trovée" (*Recueil*, III, 284).

At once a robber of robes and a blurrer of sexual difference, the poet embodies the everpresent figure of the transvestite. "*Li abis ne fait pas l'ermite*"—so begins Rutebeuf's "De Frere Denise," a tale of transvestism bound to the learning of letters and to sexual desire.[31] Thus the *frere meneur*, who is simultaneously a "brother of minor orders" and a "misleader," entices Denise to join his monastery. Tonsured, she takes the garb of a monk and like Heloise is seduced by "lessons": "Cil qui la glose li devoit / Faire entendre de sa leson, / La mist en male soupeson."[32]

The great medieval drama of poetry and transvestism is *Le Roman de Silence*, a work which in many places reads like a vernacular version of the *De Planctu Naturae*. *Natura formatrix* stands for the principle of difference, and her creation of the heroine is explicitly linked to writing: "Les orelles le fait petites / Nature ki les a escrites, / Les sorcils brun et bien seöir, / Nul hom ne puet si bials veöir."[33] Nature's work, however, has been perverted ("Que s'uevre li ont bestornee" [*Silence*, v. 2259]) by the travesty of a proper name. Her parents, in order to insure her inheritance of the paternal duchy, and against the royal prohibition of such a transfer to a woman, attempt to cover the scandal of her sexual identity with a false appellation. As her father Cador confesses to his wife Eufemie, whose own name suggests euphemistic inflation, the suffix of their daughter's name is against nature and natural usage:

> Il iert només Scilenscius;
> Et s'il avient par aventure

> Al descovrir de sa nature
> Nos muerons cest -us en -a,
> S'avra a non Scilencia.
> Se nos li tolons dont cest -us
> Nos li donrons natural us,
> Car cis -us est contre nature,
> Mais l'altres seroit par nature.
>
> > (*Silence*, v. 2074)

She will be named 'Scilencius'; and if it happens by chance that her true nature is discovered, we will change this -*us* into -*a*, and his name will be 'Scilencia.' If we remove then this -*us*, we restore to her her natural law; for this -*us* is imposed against nature, but the other is by nature.

Silence considers herself a "sophism of Nature" ("Dont se porpense en lui meïsme / Que Nature li fait sofime" [*Silence*, v. 2539]), as the -*us* that is against both custom ("Por che que l'us est encontre us" [*Silence*, v. 2541]) and nature ("Car cis us n'est pas natureus" [*Silence*, v. 2554]) comes to constitute the gap—or specific minimal difference—within which this drama of language and lineage is played out.

To borrow Alain's terms, the *Roman de Silence* represents an occulted attempt to transform poetry into grammar, or to recuperate the oxymoronic impossibility of the hermaphrodite—the "malle de femiele," the "vallés meschine" (*Silence*, vv. 2041, 3763)—by the straightness of a proper imposition. And it offers at the same time a good indication of how the romance author writing in the high period of the fabliaux conceived of the undertaking of poetry itself.

Silence is the figure of the poet. Raised in isolation (a medieval Wild Child), she becomes aware, around the time of puberty, not only that she is a female "trapped in the clothes of a male," but that she is inextricably attracted to poetry, specifically to a troupe of jongleurs with whom she escapes. The transvestite performer becomes synonymous with a systematic refusal of univocal meaning. A multiform creature like Jean's Faux-Semblant, the Sanson of "Richeut," or Merlin, whom she captures, Silence is the liar, the deceiver and trickster—a "bel semblant" (*Silence*, v. 5001) who wears other clothes and takes other names in defiance of Nature's rule of difference: "Car cil a fait de son non cange, / Si l'a mué por plus estrange" (*Silence*, v. 3175). Silence embodies the pluralistic possibilities of fiction and assumes its multiple functions.

The *Roman de Silence* revolves around the attempt to bring the suffix -*a* into consonance with the identity of its bearer: "Silence atornent come feme / . . . Ostés est -us, mis i est -a / Si est només Silentia" (*Silence*, v. 6664). And it is about the attempt to bring the inappropriate clothes that obscure a female anatomy ("Il est desos les dras mescine" [*Silence*, v. 2480]) into line with the body. A proper garment and a proper name restore the rule of nature, or sexual difference:

> Segnor, que vos diroie plus?
> Ains ot non Scilensiüs
> Ostés est -us, mis i est -a,
> Si est només Scilentiä.
> D'illuec al tierc jor que Nature
> Ot recovree sa droiture
> Si prist Nature a repolir
> Par tolt li cors et a tolir
> Tolt quanque ot sor le cors de male.
>
> (*Silence*, v. 6665)

My Lords, what more can I tell? Thus she lost the name Scilensiüs: the -*us* was taken away and the -*a* restored, and she was named Scilentiä. The third day after Nature had recovered her right (straightness) she began to rework the body and to remove any traces of masculinity.

With Silence's assumption of her name the text assumes its name, and the author is reduced literally to silence: "Segnor, que vos diroie plus?" Properly named, the transvestite's donning of an appropriate dress is tantamount to a reduction of fiction's infinite possibilities to univocal meaning—a univocity that precludes further narrative progression.

More the rule than the exception, the condition of the transvestite is that of the poet whose search for an appropriate garb is synonymous with the search for meaning that is the precondition of narrative. The poet wears the clothes of the Other; he is a trader in cloth. Indeed, given the little that we know about the external conditions of literary performance in the High Middle Ages, the constant exchange of coats (tails?) for tales represents an important element of the textual economy of an era in which—especially in the regions the fabliaux come from and refer to—textiles were the prime commodity.[34] The jongleurs of *Erec et Enide* are rewarded with robes. Jouglet, the poet of *Guillaume de Dole*, receives a mantle as payment for his image of Lïenor; the Emperor Conrad, because of his desire for that image and for poems, is divested piece-by-piece of his clothes.[35] But nowhere is the exchange of clothes for song more visible than in the fabliaux. On the level of theme, it is emblematic of the poet's relation to others (performers, patrons, and public), of his status, and finally, of the poem itself.

The economy of clothes and poetry in the fabliaux is closed. The circulation of poems is inextricably linked to that of the textile goods for which they are exchanged and into which, as also suggested in "La Vieille Truande," they are so readily transformed. "It is the business of jongleurs and magicians to acquire the robes of knights"—so claims the author of "Le Chevalier à la robe vermeille."[36] And it is through "a new scarlet robe" that the rapport between poet and patron is negotiated in "Du Vilain au buffet":

> Li quens manda les menestrels,
> Et si a fet crier entr'els
> Qui la meillor truffe sauroit
> Dire ne fere, qu'il auroit
> Sa robe d'escarlate nueve.
> L'uns menestrels à l'autre rueve
> Fere son mestier tel qu'il sot;
> L'un fet l'ivre, l'autres le sot
> L'uns chante, li autres note,
> Et li autres dit la riote,
> Et li autres la jenglerie;
> Cil qui sevent de jouglerie
> Vielent par devant le conte,

> Aucuns i a qui fabliaus conte,
> Où il ot mainte gaberie,
> Et li autres dit l'*Erberie*
> Là où il ot mainte risée.
>
> (*Recueil*, III, 203)

The count sent for his minstrels and had it proclaimed that the one who had the best act—whether speaking or mime—would have his new scarlet robe. One minstrel challenged another to do his trade as he knew it. One played the drunk, the other the fool; one sang, the other strummed; another performed the "Dit de la riote"; and another la jenglerie ["La Contregengle"?]. Those who knew the jongleur's art strummed in front of the count. Some told fabliaux in which there is many a trick, others the "Dit de l'Erberie" in which there are many chuckles.

Just as in the courtly lyric the poet courts his lord's wife, he seeks in the fabliaux to relieve the lord of his coat. The robe is assimilable to poetic performance. And not to just any performance, for the poet's repertoire includes not only fabliaux, but precisely the *dits* with which we began the present study— that is, the "Dit de la riote" or "de l'Erberie," of which the "Rencontre du Roi d'Angleterre et du jongleur d'Ely" is a version.

The coat exchanged for poetry becomes the outward sign of talent and of social status. As the author of "De Saint Piere et du jongleur" observes, nudity, want of an instrument, and a lack of artistic reputation or name go hand-in-hand:

> Il ot un jouglor à Sens
> Qui mout ert de povre riviere,
> N'avoit pas sovent robe entiere.
> Ne sai comment on l'apele,
> Mais souvent as dez se pela;
> Sovent estoit sanz sa viele,
> Et sanz chauces et sanz cotele,
> Si que au vent et à la bise
> Estoit sovent en sa chemise.
>
> (*Recueil*, V, 65)

There was a jongleur at Sens who was of small reputa-
tion; he didn't have a complete suit. I do not know his
name, but he often lost his shirt at dice. Often he was
without his viol, and without shoes and without a coat,
so that in all kinds of weather he was in shirt-sleeves.

The fabliaux that turn around accusations and counteraccusa-
tions, insults, and jibes exchanged between rival poets contain
the obligatory reference to clothes that are the equivalent of
poetic skill. "Never, ever, did he receive a new robe for any-
thing he says," taunts one of the ribalds of "Des Deux Bor-
deors ribauz"; and his counterpart of "La Contregengle"
claims "to have seen his rival in many a court wearing clothes
worth 3 soldes. . . . He doesn't have much of a reputation as
do other minstrels who receive robes and belong to great
entourages."[37]

To what extent is the regularized exchange of poems for
clothes as the emblem of a mediated relation between poet and
patron different from the theft of clothes?

The "Dit des marchéans," one of the numerous *dits* in-
cluded among the fabliaux, gives some indication of how to
go about answering this question. Thus the author, pretend-
ing to pray for the protection of merchants against those who
steal their clothes—"Et des larrons, Diex, les gardez / Que il
ne soient desrobez"—at the same time seeks merely to be the
first to prey upon them: "Et les marchéandes aussi / N'i met
Phelippot en oubli" (*Recueil*, II, 128). Feigning a common in-
terest with the merchant, Phelippot complains of having been
robbed of his clothes ("Et il les deffend du dé / Qui maintes
foiz m'a desrobé"), while he dresses to rob again:

> Se Dieu plest je m'enroberai
> Et aus marchéanz conterai
> Des diz noviaus si liement
> Qu'il me donront de lor argent.
>
> (*Recueil*, II, 128)

And if it please God, I will dress and for merchants sing
new *dits* so that they will give me their money.

By placing himself rhetorically in the position of the Same the poet assumes the role of the Other, which suggests ultimately the identity of the poet as rober and as robber.

The fabliaux are rooted in scandal—in theft, bastardy, sodomy, sophistry, deceit, and prostitution; they insist incessantly that the coat of representation is to some degree always ill-fitting, always dirty and torn. "Shouldn't you have a coat that is whole?" asks the poet of his rival in "La Contregengle"; "you should be a hauler (*hote*) of excrement and carry manure in two baskets."[38] As the ambiguity of the word "hote" (*hotte*) implies, the poet is both entertainer and hod; poetry is assimilable to excrement. Here we encounter the fabliau entitled "De Jouglet," or "The Jongleur," in which the high seriousness of a marriage between the son of a rich vilaine and an impoverished knight's daughter is set against the shenanigans of the poet:

> La vielle charga Robinet
> Son fil .I. menestrel Jouglet
> Que il au moustier le menast
> Et apreïst et enseignast,
> Qu'il estoit sages et soutieus
> Et ses filz estoit enfantieus.
>
> (*Recueil*, IV, 114)

The old woman entrusted her son Robin to Jouglet, a minstrel who was to take him to church and teach him the ways of the world since he was wise and her son only a naive child.

The wisdom of the poet turns out to be that of the practical joker, for Jouglet's advice is to eat vast quantities of green apples and never to defecate on one's wedding day (a pun upon the French expression "fermer le robinet"?): "Sachiez que l'en ne chie mie / Le jor c'on espeuse s'amie / Quar ce seroit trop grant ledure."[39]

Robin, as ignorant of sexuality as he is of the jongleur's wiles, confesses to his wife, "Je muir de chier." And eventually he defecates everywhere—in the water closet, in the clothes closet, in the fireplace, in the bucket used for washing, in Jouglet's bed, his clothes, his hair, hands, mouth, and worst of all, in his harp case and viol (*Recueil*, IV, 121–25):

> Mès encore fu ce neenz
> Envers ce qu'ele li fist fere,
> Quar la viele li fist trere
> Qui estoit pendue au postel;
> Se li fist chier el forrel. . . .
>
> (*Recueil*, IV, 121)

But this was nothing compared to what she [Robin's wife] had him do, for she had him fetch the viol hanging on a post, and he excreted into the case.

In the equation of fiction making and excrement making, the circularity of the trouvère's trick ("Jouglet qui la borde trueve" [*Recueil*, IV, 115]) thus becomes the equivalent of a natural or moral law: "Qui merde brasse, merde boive" (IV, 119); "Teus cuide cunchier autrui / Qui tout avant cunchie lui" (IV, 127).[40]

This world filled with or transformed into excrement mirrors precisely what Jouglet does when he causes everything to pass through the bowels of Robin, or assimilates everything to the poem. And it is finally no different from the universe of "De Audigier," the epic of excrement first published in the Méon/Barbazan collection of fabliaux and of which LeClerc affirms that "personne aujourd'hui n'oserait citer la description" (FL, p. 196).

The "soft kingdom" of Audigier's father is that of the intestine "in which people are buried in excrement up to their neck."[41] And if the monumental nuptial bowel movement of "De Jouglet" is the result of the jongleur's wiles, a similar obsession defines even the courtship of the hero's parents: Turgibus is seduced by the charms of Rainberge—her prunes, their pits, and the wiping of her posterior parts on his "beautiful scarlet coat":

> Rainberge fu issue de sa maison,
> Qui n'avoit a cel ore point de Baron:
> Vers le vassal s'en torne à estupon,

Si li a tot montré le cul et con.
Venez avant, fet-ele, filz a Baron,
Acroupez-vos lez moi et si chion.
Ge mengai ersoir prunes à grant foison,
Si me saillent du cul li noeillon,
Ne ge n'ai aporté point de torchon:
Vos avez bele cote de vermeillon,
Forbissez m'en le cul à cel giron. . . .

(*Fabliaux et contes*, IV:218)

Rainberge, who at that time had no husband, came out of her house. She turned squatting toward the vassal and showed him her ass and cunt. "Come here," she said, "son of a baron; squat down beside me and let's shit. Last night I ate a load of prunes, and the pits are coming out of my ass. I didn't bring anything to wipe with, but you have a beautiful scarlet coat; wipe my ass with the lap of it. . . .

Not only does the marital gift consist of 15 dog turds ("De quinze estrons de chien li fist doaire"), but the nuptial meal is composed of fresh cheese on stale dung: "Les napes estendirent sor estrons sès, / Et enprès si mengerent fromaiges frès" (*Fabliaux et contes*, IV:219). So too Audigier "takes his betrothed by the mantle . . . and, shitting, places a ring on her finger." His own marriage feast consists of "a good stew mixed with chicken droppings," after which the jongleurs are each paid "30 turds from a goat."[42]

The scandal attached to the dirty coat of fiction—whether that of Jouglet or of Turgibus—is, finally, that of coprophagy, which is common to the excremental hero ("Et quant il ot chiié plaine s'aumuce, / Ses doiz boute en la merde, puis se les suce" [*Fabliaux et contes*, IV:217]) and his son: "Audigier, dit Guiberge, bouse vos di, / De trois de mes estrons et demi / Vous desgéuneroiz demain matin" (*Fabliaux et contes*, IV:227).

The ingestion of excrement is, in fact, the theme of a fabliau entitled "De la Crote." "Sister," says the peasant, opening his fly, "guess what I hold in my hand?"[43] His wife assumes it is his penis ("Je cuit que ce est vostre andoille") and is proved wrong: "Par mon chief, ainçois est ma coille" (*Re-*

cueil, III, 47). Seeking to venge herself, she reaches under her dress; and, withdrawing a piece of excrement "a little larger than a pea," she challenges him to continue the game.[44] After he looks and guesses pâté, she invites him to feel it; he feels it and guesses wax, and she invites him to taste it; he tastes it ("Cil en sa bouche dedenz / La met et masche entre ses denz") and not wanting to lose the bet, he exclaims: " 'Par le cuer bieu . . . c'est merde' " (*Recueil*, III, 48).

It was, I admit, a reading of "De la Crote" against widespread claims of the fabliaux's so-called "historical" or "social realism" that first set in motion the train of thought leading to the present book.[45] As a presentation of "the way things really were" in the thirteenth century, as a "window" upon the medieval world, does this tale mean that peasant couples in northern France exposed their genitals and tasted each other's excrement to chase away the boredom of long winter nights? Probably not. What it does suggest, however, is a consciousness on the part of the poet of the relationship between the theme and function of the fabliau, or between the turd of "De la Crote" and the tale's power to amuse. Such a reading is inferred from the beginning in the promise of a "short piece" ("fable cort et petit") whose subject is synonymous with small pieces. And it is evident in the clever wife's "finding of a turd"—"Si a trové une crote"—that is the equivalent of her "inventing," "composing," or "singing of" a turd.[46] The inventive woman is, in other words, an inscription of the poet in the work whose turd-like compression transforms the project of poetry into a closed circuit between the anus and the mouth and that hints, ultimately, at what it means to ingest and excrete that which already has been ingested and excreted.

The reabsorption of the already absorbed is, in fact, the point of departure of "De la Crote." "Commencier vous vueil un fablel, / Por ce qu'il m'est conté et dit . . ." (*Recueil*, III, 46)—so begins the poet who, rather than stress the originality of his material, insists instead upon its supervenient and supplementary nature. And he is not alone, for the jongleurs of the fabliaux, more than any other group of performers (or poets) in an age beholden to authority, admit to receiving their material from elsewhere: "J'oï conter l'autre semaine"

(*Recueil*, III, 68); "Jehans li Galois nous raconte" (III, 88); "Nos trovomes en escriture" (III, 209); "Ot-on maintes choses conter / Qui bones sont a raconter" (I, 82); "Un exemple vueil conmencier / Qu'apris de Monseigneur Rogier" (I, 194); "Une fable vueil comencer, / Que j'oy l'autr'er conter" (II, 193); "Une aventure molt petite / Qui n'a mie esté sovent dite / Ai oï dire, tot por voir, / Que je vos voil ramentevoir" (V, 43); "Voudré je un fabliau ja fere / Dom la matiere oï retrere / A Vercelai devant les changes" (V, 151).[47]

The list of *incipits* claiming (not confessing) derivation is almost coterminous with the fabliaux. And if the above examples are only a random sample, they nonetheless make the point that the comic tale is composed by the assimilation of another's material and its reexpression. Or, as in the case of "Boivin de Provins," by the discharge of one's own repeated duty:

> Boivin s'en vint droit au provost:
> Se li a conté mot à mot
> De chief en chief la verité.
> Et li provos l'a escouté,
> Qui mout ama la lecherie;
> Sovent li fist conter sa vie
> A ses parens, à ses amis,
> Qui mout s'en sont joué et ris.
>
> (*Recueil*, V, 64)

Boivin went straight to the provost: he told him the truth word for word from beginning to end. And the provost, who loved tales of lechery, listened. He made him tell his life story often to his relatives and friends, who were greatly amused and laughed.

Ultimately, even the tale that is supposedly invented—recounted "from life" and for the first time—becomes, through repetition, nonessential and collateral: "Se li dona de ses deniers / Li provos .X. sous à BOIVINS, / Qui cest fablel fist à Provins" (*Recueil*, V, 64).

Ménard claims that the place of excrement in the fabliaux is "completely marginal," and "leaving *Jouglet* aside . . . , the rest of these texts present only rare traces of such inspiration": "Quant à la scatologie, elle n'apparaît que dans trois ou quatre textes."[48] The scholar's attempt to wash away the scandal of scatology is not, however, as simple as it seems.[49] Besides being central to such diverse tales as "De la Dame qui Aveine demandoit por Morel sa provende avoir," "De Porcelet," "De Jouglet," "Le Vilain Asnier," "Charlot le juif qui chia dans un pel de lièvre," "De Audigier," "De la Crote," *inter alia*, the centrality of excrement to the poetic enterprise is assured precisely because of its marginality. As *disjectus*, it is what jonglerie is all about.

The jongleur circulates and recirculates dead—fecal, inert—matter: "Tu trueves ainz c'on ait perdu" (*Recueil*, II, 261), inveighs the poet of "La Contregengle," who assimilates jonglerie to plagiarism:

> Mès tu ne sez nule rien dire;
> Tu ne fez rien fors d'autrui lire. . . .
> Quanque tu as ici jenglé
> As tu d'autre leu descenglé;
> Je suis près de ce prover
> Que tu m'as ci oï conter.
>
> (*Recueil*, II, 262)

But you don't know how to say anything; all you do is read others. . . . Whatever you have sung here you stole from another. I know how to prove that you heard me sing it.

In condemning his rival the poet indicts himself—and thus brings us full circle. For if, as the jongleur asserts, poetry is theft, then there can be no distinction between the pilfering of coats and of poetic material. "So help you God," the poet asks, "where did you steal that overcoat you are wearing?":[50]

> Or emble tant que tu porras;
> Por .I. pendre quites seras.
> Trop par esprens à .I. besoing;
> Tu n'as de l'autrui chose soing,
> Se nel pues tolir ou embler.
>
> (*Recueil*, II, 261)

Now you steal all you can; you will pay for it by hanging. You are obsessed by one thing; you don't care about anything you cannot steal or rob.

What this means is that when poets "steal the pants off each other" or "rob the robes" of patrons, they merely alert us to the premise underlying the practice of poetry in the High Middle Ages—that is, the circulation of a limited number of texts that, always already stolen, belong to no one, are common property, and in fact, as dead letters, are living proof of the literary text as a system of self-creating value.

What is the closed corpus that the jongleur circulates and recirculates? We get a good indication in "Les Deux Bordeors ribauz":

> Cantères sui qu'el mont n'a tel:
> Ge sai de Guillaume au tinel,
> Si com il arriva as nés,
> Et de Renouart au cort nés
> Sai-ge bien chanter com ge vueil,
> Et si sai d'Aïe de Nantueil
> Si com ele fu en prison;
> Si sai de Garins d'Avignon,
> Qui moult estore bon romans;
> Si sai de Guion d'Aleschans
> Et de Vivien de Bourgogne;
> Si sai de Bernart de Saisoigne
> Si sai de Guiteclin de Brebant;
> Si sai d'Ogier de Montaubant,
> Si com il conquist Ardennois;
> Si sai de Renaut le Danois.

> (*Recueil*, I, 3–4)

I am the best singer in the world. I know William with the stick, and how it happened to his nose. And about Renouart with the short nose I know how to sing as I will. I know Aïe de Nanteuil and how she was in prison; I know Garins d'Avignon, which makes a good story. I know Guion d'Aleschans, and all about Vivien de Bourgogne; and I know about Bernart de Saisoigne and Guiteclin de Brabant; and I know Ogier of Montaubant and how he conquered the Ardennes; I know about Renaut le Danois.

And, moving to the romance:

> Ge sai des romanz d'aventure,
> De cels de la réonde Table,
> Qui sont à oïr delitable.
> De Gauvain sai le mal parler
> Et de Quex le bon chavalier;
> Si sai de Perceval de Blois;
> De Pertenoble le Galois
> Sai ge plus de .XL. laisses.
>
> (*Recueil*, I, 4)

I know romances of adventure of those of the Round Table, which are so pleasing to hear. I know about Gauvain's evil tongue and about Quex the brave knight; I know the one about Perceval de Blois; and of Pertenoble le Galois I know more than 40 laisses.

Here is the ultimate literary source—the jongleur's own testimony regarding the repertoire of the thirteenth-century performer.

But what is such an inventory? A list that in its confusions rivals even the most disappointing doctoral exam. For Renouart au Tinel we get Renouart au cort nés; and for Guillaume au Court Nez, Guillaume au Tinel. For Aye d'Avignon (who was in prison) we get Aïe de Nanteuil; and for Garnier de Nanteuil, Garins d'Avignon; for Vivien d'Aleschan, Guion d'Aleschans; and for Gui de Bourgogne, Vivien de Bourgogne. For Bernart de Brabant we find Guiteclin de Brebant; and for Guiteclin de Sassoigne (or de Saxe), Bernart de Saisoigne. Ogier le Danois is conflated with Renaut de Montauban. And, shifting to the romance, the roles of Gauvain the Brave and Quex the Malevolent are reversed, as are the names of Perceval le Galois and Partenopeu de Blois.

Only the most literal-minded scholar would take seriously such a parodic inventory; and there is always one. "Il y a là de quoi exercer longtemps quiconque voudra retrouver enfin les annales complètes de l'ancienne musique française," writes LeClerc (FL, p. 96). Yet the fabliau's mock epic format indicates a more serious point: nowhere do the fabliaux lead to the kind of certainty that historically has been demanded of them. The outlandishly jumbled claims of the rival jongleurs are, in other words, a tip-off to something operative within the genre as a whole—the opacity of even the most realistic *seeming* text and the gratuity of the historian's quest for univocal meaning.

The poet is by his own admission a maker of useless objects, and especially clothes ("reins for cows," "gloves for dogs," "hats for goats," "hauberks for hares").[51] He is a doer of useless deeds ("a roofer with tarts," "a bleeder of cats," "a leecher of steers," "a beater of eggs").[52] And, what is more, there can be no distinction between such absurdly superfluous tasks and the project of poetry itself: "I make good sheaths for tripods and good cases for scythes; and if I had two harps, I would not let pass the chance to sing such a song as you have never heard."[53]

Thus the fabliaux may exhibit more naked bodies than any other medieval genre and indeed may introduce a foretaste of Bakhtin's "celebration of lower body parts"; but they are not to be confused with the naked body of Nature. On the contrary, they are as bound by the ill-fitting garments of representation as even the most hermetic form. There is, for example, no essential difference between the jongleur's pretending to be a "glover of dogs," an "armorer of hares," or a "beater of eggs," and the troubadour Marcabru's boast of being "filled with an infinity of artifices, with a hundred means of achieving my goal (or harming). On the one side, I carry fire, and on the other, I carry the water to put it out."[54] Marcabru brags of "making words full of breaks," just as Raimbaut d'Aurenga boasts of "intertwining rare, dark, and obscure words."[55] So too Bernart Marti claims to be so crafty in his "mixing of words" that he succeeds in the "mixing of things."[56] Nor, finally, can one distinguish between the absurd posturing of the jongleur of the fabliaux and William IX's claim to have composed a *vers* "while asleep, and walking, and standing in the sun."[57] Both render explicit the extent to which the garment of fiction is itself always already rent.

CHAPTER 2

THE BODY AND ITS PARTS

Senis officiis seni privantur et uno,
Vel nulli nullo coeunt lare nulla loquentes.
Qui cecus "video"; qui surdus hic "audeo fures";
Qui mutus "clamemus" ait; truncus "fugiamus,"
Mancus "pugnemus"; qui naris "odoror" obesae;
Hic "dulces escas comedamus" qui sine gustu.
Ex aliquo nihil est, ex re privatio rursus.
Est aliquid tamen ex nichilo si fabula malit:
Sic nulli fures, sic nulli qui coiere;
Sic in re nulla sermonem collige nullum,
Sicut rem, sermo sermonem, res probat esse.

FULCOIUS (11TH CENTURY)

(Seven men are deprived of seven senses; and none of
them, saying nothing, assembles in no house. The blind
one says, "I see thieves"; the deaf one says, "I hear
them." The mute cries, "Let us call for help"; the man
missing a leg, "Let us flee." The man missing an arm
says, "Let us fight"; he whose nose is not quick "I can
smell them"; and the one with no taste, "Let us eat
sweet things." From something there is nothing, from
something a nothing in return. But from nothing there
is something, if the story should have it: thus there are
no thieves, thus there is none who assembles. Thus in
nothing you acquire no story; just as something proves
that something is, a story a story.)

In the preceding chapter we explored a few examples of one of
the most poignant paradigms of representation in the Middle
Ages—the representation of representation as a garment or
coat. The poetic sign maintains a relation to that which it sig-
nifies—Nature—analogous to the relation between the body
and its clothes. This way of thinking about symbolic activity

is, further, evident across a wide range of generic types, both Latin and vernacular, and including the allegory, lyric, and romance. It is particularly well developed in the fabliaux where it comes to constitute the prime metaphor for an entire literary mode. Beginning with the "riotous fable," we arrived at the "textile text" only to discover, however, that the comic tale often seems to cover-up more than to cover. The robe of fiction is to some degree always inadequate to the body. It carries the odor of scandal. This scandal is thematized in a variety of ways—as theft, or stolen coats; as perversion, especially sodomy; as transvestism, adultery, trickery, prostitution; as excrement and as coprophagy, which is linked to a conception of poetry as plagiarism. Moral dereliction expressed at the thematic level is, moreover, only the most visible sign of the underlying scandal of the fabliaux, which is that of poetry itself.

But what about the body beneath the ill-fitting garment of fiction? Is there a meaningful reality beyond fiction, an "outside" of the text that is not text and might somehow escape the limits as well as the scandal of representation? Is it possible to conceive of a stable point of reference against which the fabliaux might be considered to be particularly transgressive? Given the degraded nature of all signs, can such a point have substantive or ontological existence? Put another way, is it possible to produce, or even to imagine, a nonscandalous text?

The response to these questions is admittedly overdetermined by all that has occurred in the last 25 years in the realm of literary criticism, philosophy, the social sciences, the humanities, and in particular, by the radical reexamination of the relation between such traditionally independent disciplines. It is, therefore, the answer of a reader of the 1980s and not the 1880s. And it is "no." For if the cloak of fiction is always ill-fitting, always torn, dirtied, and inadequate to cover that which it merely covers up, the body itself is also never whole. Just as the jongleur's repertoire is confused and corrupt, the body within the fabliaux is fragmented. Naked Nature, that which the garment of representation supposedly covers, is merely another representation that is partial and disjointed.

Here we touch upon the ubiquitous theme of dismember-
ment and castration. In the Middle Ages bodily mutilation
was almost always treated in larger than physical terms and is
linked implicitly to the field of sacramental theology and the
relation of each Christian to the Church and to the body of
Christ. I have maintained elsewhere that Abelard's mutilation,
for example, is intimately bound to the legendary castrato's
linguistic theory, theology, and to the global project of philos-
ophy itself. Or, as we have seen in the case of *Le Roman de la
rose*, Jean de Meun problematizes the question of verbal sig-
nification around the debate over how to name that which Sat-
urn lost at the time of his castration.[1]

Within the fabliaux detached sexual organs circulate as
freely as the detachable meanings contained in the disparate
plagiarized repertoire of the jongleur.

A few examples. In "Du Pescheor du pont sur Saine" a
marital dispute over the importance of sex in marriage culmi-
nates in the wife's disparaging of her husband's member ("Ce
est la riens qui plus m'anuie" [*Recueil*, III, 70]). While fishing
in the Seine the next day he comes upon a dead priest still in a
tumescent state. Severing the erect organ and placing it in his
creel, he presents it to his wife who sues for divorce before
submitting to him. In "De .III. Dames qui troverent .I. vit"
the quarrel over which of three pilgrims will keep a male or-
gan found along their pilgrimage route ("Que .II. coiz et .I.
vit mout gros / Troverent, où il n'ot point d'os" [*Recueil*, V,
32]) is resolved by a clever abbess who pretends to recognize
in it the abbey's stolen door-knocker. In "Du Prestre crucifié"
a sculptor or maker of religious images comes home to find
his wife with her priest-lover. Unsure about where to flee, the
priest takes off his clothes, mounts a cross, and hides among
the crosses in the workroom ("Entre les ymages de fust / S'es-
tent ausi come s'il en fust" [*Recueil*, I, 195]). The husband
meanwhile decides to inspect his recent creations and, as-
tonished at the sloppiness of his work, trims what he deli-
cately refers to as a bit of "excess material": "Que vit et coilles
li trencha, / Que onques riens ne li lessa" (*Recueil*, I, 196).

In "Du Prestre crucifié" the exchange of testicles for "the

love of another's wife" is as natural as the exchange of the priest's money for his life:

> Cest example nous monstre bien
> Que nus prestres por nule rien
> Ne devroit autrui fame amer,
> N'entor li venir ne aler,
> Quiconques fust en calengage,
> Que il n'i lest ou coille ou gage,
> Si come fist cil prestres Constans,
> Qui i lessa les siens pendans.
>
> (*Recueil*, I, 197)

This example shows us well that a priest should under no circumstances love another's wife, nor come around her. Whoever disputes this must leave his balls as collateral as did Prestre Constans who left his hanging there.

Prestre Constans is a constant within the fabliaux. We find his equivalent in "Du Prestre et du leu" (V, 51), "Aloul" (I, 225), "Le Povre Clerc" (V, 192), "Du Prestre teint" (VI, 22), and in "De Connebert" where a jealous blacksmith fastens his wife's lover's testicles to the anvil, thus forcing his self-mutilation:

> Se li prestres tant sa coille aime
> Qu'il ne la cope ne ne tranche,
> Ne l'avra que la mort ne sante; . . .
> Car il em prist en tel meniere
> Qu'il i laissa les .II. coillons
> Autresi granz con .II. roignons.
> La pel est si grant et si rosse
> Q'an en poïst faire une borsse.
>
> (*Recueil*, V, 168–69)

If the priest loves his balls so much that he will not cut them, then he will lose his life; . . . For he acted in such a way as to leave behind his two balls as big as kidneys. The skin is so big and red that one could make a purse out of it.

Ménard estimates the number of fabliaux involving unfaithful women to constitute fully one third of the corpus (FM, p. 14);

and as Nykrog notes, "in such triangles the lover is *always* a priest" (FN, p. 62). To complete the syllogism one might add that the priest is almost always dismembered—castrated, beaten, or killed—for his concupiscence.

So general is the theme of mutilation within the fabliaux that women are separated from their sexual organs as frequently as men. In *Trubert*, for example, the trickster-hero castrates a woman and presents her genitals to the Duke as his enemy's nostrils and mouth: "Le cul et le con li coupa, / En s'aloiere le bouta . . . / 'Sire,' dit il, 'la bouche i est / de Goulias et les narilles'."[2] And, in what remains the most outrageous (and interesting) example of female mutilation, "De la Dame escolliée," we encounter the tale of a son-in-law's mock castration of his wife's domineering mother, which serves as a means of bringing the entire household under paternal law.

Dismemberment is not, however, necessarily thematized as castration. Detached sexual organs are an integral part of the representation of the body in the fabliaux and are more the rule than the exception. "Le Souhaiz desvez" recounts the story of a sexually frustrated wife who dreams one night of a "marché au vits" where phalluses are sold "both retail and wholesale" at prices ranging from 10 sous for a small one, to 30 for a "good one," to 50 for a "magnificent one."[3] The companion piece to "Le Souhaiz desvez" is entitled "Du Moine" and recounts the dream of an abstinent monk turned loose in a market where female genitalia are sold: "Ains est toute li feste plaine / Et tous li marchiés pourtendus / De haions et de cons fendus."[4]

Both actual castration and the motif of the detached member are limit cases of a more general fetishization of body parts within the fabliaux. And yet, it is not necessary for the fetishized organ to be detached from the whole, as the series of tales that center on an attached but isolated part make abundantly clear. The author of "Du Fevre de Creeil," for example, focuses so obsessively on the blacksmith's apprentice's member that the entire body is reduced to an enormous phallus:

> Le vallés avoit non Gautiers;
> Moult est deboneres et frans,

Les rains larges, grailes les flans,
Gros par espaules et espès,
Et si portoit du premier mès
Qu'il covient aus dames servir,
Quar tel vit portoit, sans mentir,
Qui moult ert de bele feture,
Quar toute i ot mise sa cure
Nature qui formé l'avoit;
Devers le retenant avoit
Plain poing de gros et .II. de lonc. . .

(*Recueil*, I, 231)

The youth's name was Gautiers. He was quite congenial and simple, with large loins, a slim waist, and broad shoulders. And he served the first dish that one serves ladies, since he had a cock, no lie, that was perfectly formed; Nature who had made it put all her effort into it. Near the base it was a full fist wide and two long.

Here we recognize a version of the topos of *Natura formatrix*, but with one essential difference. Where elsewhere (e.g. *Erec et Enide*, *Le Roman de la rose*, *Le Roman de Silence*) the motif implies a blason of the entire body, here the body is reduced to its sexual organ; it is, in other words, castrated.

An even more striking example of the phallic body is to be found in "Les .IIII. Souhais Saint Martin." This is the story of a woodsman who, having met the benevolent Saint in the forest one day, is accorded four wishes, returns home, and is seduced by his wife into giving the first wish to her. "I request," she says, "in the name of God that you be covered with pricks. . . . One was worth nothing to me, since it was always as soft as a rag."[5] In what can only be read as a parody of the heroic catalogue of the "chanson de geste," the woodsman's body is transformed into an epic assemblage of phalluses:

Le vit le saillirent par le nez
Et par la bouche de delez;
Si ot vit lonc et vit quarré,
Vit gros, vit cort, vit reboulé,
Vit corbe, vit agu, vit gros,

Sor le vilain n'ot si dur os
Dont vit ne saillent merveillous.
Li vit li saillent des genous; . . .
Li vit li saillent des oreilles. . . .
Li sailli uns grans vit du front,
Et par aval dusques aus piez
Fu li vilains de vis chargiez. . .

(*Recueil*, V, 204)

Pricks came out of his nose and out of the side of his
mouth. He had long and square pricks, thick, short, and
fat pricks, curved and sharp pricks. There was no bone
so thick that a prick did not pop out of it. Pricks grew
on his knees . . . out of his ears . . . and a great big one
in the middle of his forehead. Up and down to his feet
he was covered with cocks.

Angered by his metamorphosis, the woodsman takes revenge
by requesting that his wife be similarly transformed;[6] and,
having both been converted into their respective sexual organs,
the woodsman seeks to rectify the situation by wishing away
their collective panoply of appendages: "Et li vilains souhaide
et dist / Qu'ele n'ait con ne il n'ait vit" (*Recueil*, V, 207). In all,
the peasant couple performs three acts of castration—two
metaphoric transformations of the body into its sexual part
and one excision of all the parts—before using the final wish
to restore to the woodsman and his wife "just one prick and
one cunt" (*Recueil*, V, 207).

The body's reduction to, or transformation into, its sexual
member culminates in a pair of fabliaux in which there can be
no distinction between the tale, its title, or the fixation upon a
single member. Thus "Le Jugement des cons" tells the story
of three sisters involved with the same man who, in order
to escape the dilemma of conflicting allegiances, promises to
marry the one who can furnish the best answer to which is
older, she or her vagina. Each is forced, in other words, to
detach her genitalia from the body; and the prize is awarded to
the one capable of greater detachment.[7] Then too, the "Dit
des cons," like the "Dit des marcheans" and the "Dit des rues

de Paris," represents a catalogue of the numerous powers and uses of the feminine sex—a paean to the female genitalia in which the tale and the tail are conflated.

A version of the dismembered body is to be found in the detached bodies whose circulation constitutes a virtual sub-genre of the Old French comic tale. Here I am thinking less of the tales in which multiple corpses are disposed of by a single individual convinced that the same dead person each time returns to life (e.g., "D'Estormi," "Les .III. Bossus") than of those in which the trajectory of a single corpse serves as a key to our understanding of dismemberment within the fabliaux. In the different versions of the story known as "Le Dit dou Soucretain" (*Recueil*, VI, 117), "Du Segretain Moine" (*Recueil*, V, 215), "Du Prestre qu'on porte" or "De la longue Nuit" (*Recueil*, IV, 1), the body of a concupiscent priest circulates throughout the neighborhood before returning to its point of origin.

In the rendering known as "Du Segretain Moine," for example, a luxurious cleric is killed by a watchful husband who disposes of the body in the monastic latrine where it is discovered by a prior who returns it to the husband's house. Astonished, the husband hides the corpse under Farmer Thibaut's manure pile in a sack in which thieves had previously placed a stolen ham. The thieves, retrieving their booty and transporting it to the tavern where they have been drinking, open the sack, discover the substitution, and return it to the hook in Thibaut's barn from which it had been stolen in the first place. Thibaut, finding a dead priest in the place of his ham, straps it to a horse which returns to the monastery, stumbles, and is ultimately blamed for the monk's death.[8] In "Du Prestre qu'on porte" the circulating body is first placed in front of the door of a neighbor, who places it on a horse, which wanders to the tenement of a peasant, who puts it in a sack, which is stolen by thieves, who return it to the beam from which they had taken a ham. The priest dressed as bacon is removed by a tavernkeeper to the bishop's linen chest where it is discovered by a prior who places it in the bishop's bed. The bishop awakens and is startled. He hits the corpse, assumes he has killed an intruder, and innocents himself by quietly burying it, just as the author acquits himself by ending—or burying—the tale: "C'onques .I. seul mot ne sonnerent. / Enfouis fu sans contredit, / Car vous arai contet et dit / .I. flablel qui n'est mie briés" (*Recueil*, IV, 40).

What is remarkable about the "tale of the long night" is the extent to which it implicates the nature of storytelling and of representation. Not only is the detached body a sign of the detached nature of signs, but the tale begins with a conscious meditation upon the potential of language for detachment or deception ("Cele, ki li cuer a mout vuele, / Pense tout el qu'ele ne die" [*Recueil*, IV, 2]); and the mobile relation of sign to meaning is stressed throughout. The tavernkeeper, perplexed by the presence of the corpse, claims not "to be so drunk as not to be able to distinguish a lantern from a bladder." Finding a priest's cape in the place of a ham, he wonders if it is a "fairy or another false semblance . . . dressed by the devil."[9] So too the thieves of "Du Segretain Moine" sense a diabolic presence behind the ham's transformation. "It is the devil," one proclaims, "who made a monk out of a ham."[10] The "devil who turns a ham into a monk" is in essence the transforming power of poetry itself—that is, the power not only to make the dead signify or speak, but to deny death by investing it with a multiplicity of forms.

The series of metamorphoses that the corpse undergoes transforms the question of how to dispose of the body into the problem of how to signify absence or death. As the lifeless body travels it alternately signifies a priest, robber, ham, linen, and knight.[11] It becomes a floating signifier whose permutations are coterminous with the tale we read. The original murderer stands as an inscription of the poet. He is an agent of change whose victim, once dead, derives its multiple meanings from the divergent contexts of the sequential attempts at disposal ("Ydoine ot non, et son seignor / Dant Guillaume le changeor" [*Recueil*, V, 215]). Like the poet, the "changeor" is the one who benefits from the exchange, recuperating as he does both the dead priest's money and the stolen ham ("Ce voldroie volentiers / Que nos eüssions les deniers" [V, 221]).

The body is a shifter. As it circulates it derives its significance from the subject with which it comes in contact, the

subject who is obliged to invest it with meaning. Where the
process becomes complicated, however, is in its very mul-
tiplicity. In meaning potentially all things to all men, the
priest—through the "change" of fiction—dies a multiple
death: "Etranglé et vif et pendu / Le trova on, tiegmoing cel
conte" (*Recueil*, IV, 39).[12] "Strangled and alive and hanged
they found him"—or *composed* him—"as the tale tells." Seen
globally, the tale both inscribes and is inscribed in a certain
impossibility of investing the body with univocal interpreta-
tion. Herein lies the scandal of the "tale of the long night."
For if the disposal of the body involves a cover-up, its circula-
tion betrays all whom it touches:

> Et li vilains mout se pena
> De celer se mesaventure,
> Qui mout estoit diverse et dure
> A chiaus sor cui ele chaï:
> Chascuns s'en tint bien à traï. . . .
>
> (*Recueil*, IV, 39)

The peasant took great pains to hide his misadventure
which was very mixed and hard on each one upon
whom it fell; for each considered himself to have been
betrayed. . . .

The body, a universal signifier by the diversity of meanings
imposed upon it, becomes the focus of universal guilt.

Before the corpse, the subject is implicitly and always al-
ready guilty. Thus the fear of the man to whose horse the
corpse is tied ("Se chis afaires est seüs, / Tous li mons me
devra huer"); the fear of the monk who finds it in the latrine
("Or dira l'on devant l'abbè / Qu'en trahison l'avrai murtri");
the fear of the prior who finds him in the linen chest ("On
dira ke je l'ai tué"); and thus the panic of the neighbors before
whose door the body is first placed ("Car on diroit, et à grant
tort, / Que por le sien l'avriemes mort").[13] As the hapless
couple laments "we are innocent, but one cannot live without
such grief," ("Sachiés ke nous n'i avons coupe; / Mais on ne
puet sans annui vivre" [*Recueil*, IV, 16]).

By the universal appropriation of guilt that it provokes, the
circulating body comes to resemble, and indeed to participate

in, the scandalous nature of the poetic sign. The couple's "On ne puet sans annui vivre" recalls the poet's lament with which we began: "Dieus! Que le siecle est maloré / Quant on ne peut vivre sans estre blamé." And if one is always already guilty before the circulating corpse, it is because one is obliged to invest it with a meaning that is, by definition, partial, twisted, self-indicting, and improper. Like the dead body, the body of representation is rooted in a deforming illegitimacy—in this case the scandal of adulterous desire, robbery, and obfuscation. As the robbers, themselves trying to hide the guilt for murder behind that of theft, claim:

> Nous ne savons dont il nous vient,
> Et nonporquant bien me souvient,
> .I. bacon el saic nous mesismes,
> Quant nous l'anblames et presimes."
> (*Recueil*, IV, 24)

We don't know where he comes from, but I can remember that we put a ham in the sack after we stole and walked off with it.

The scandal of the "tale of the long night" is finally that of representation itself. Dead, the body, like the letter, engenders a series of imperfect meanings, each of which implicates the one who interprets (and who fears interpretation) in a cover-up whose origin can never be known. Such a conclusion is built into "Du Segretain Moine." The money that Guillaume "the changer" takes from the priest whom he kills (because of the cleric's concupiscence) merely recuperates his own losses at the hands of highwaymen who rob—literally "disrobe"—him of the cloth he has brought to market to sell (*Recueil*, V, 216).

This scandalous interpretation of the tales of the detached body as a parable of scandalous interpretation brings us back to the wider implications of dismemberment within the fabliaux. For if everyone with whom the corpse comes into contact is obliged to invest it with a necessarily scandalous meaning, to implicate him or herself in the act of reading the body, it is poetic language finally that condemns and is condemned. The dismemberment of the body is in other words directly associated with the modes of linguistic disruption that are the essence of the fabliaux. These are multiple—ranging from phonological, onomastic, or semantic misunderstandings, to the elaborate use of proverbs and extended metaphor, verbal automatism, and finally, to bilingualism.[14]

"De la Male Honte," for example, focuses on the mixup between a trunk belonging to a man named Honte and the notion of shame. The executor of Honte's will tries to deliver a coffer containing the dead man's wordly goods to the king. "La male Honte vos aporte" (*Recueil*, IV, 42), he says three times and each time is rebuffed. Finally, having understood the error, the king accepts the legacy which makes him part of the jongleur's joke: "Ainsi ot cil la male Honte" (IV, 46). The dead man's trunk is, in other words, a version of the circulating corpse. Repeatedly rejected, it carries blame wherever it lands.

"Estula," the tale of a stolen stole, turns around an onomastic confusion similar to that of "De la Male Honte." Here a priest is summoned to interpret what a farmer believes to be the miracle of a talking dog when, in fact, the miracle is that of ventriloquy—displaced speech. The farmer's son, calling their dog's name, "Estula," is misunderstood by a thief in hiding who hears "Es tu là?" and responds "Oïl voirement, sui je ci" (*Recueil*, IV, 89). The fragmentation of the proper name is linked to the priest's fear of bodily dismemberment, which accounts for his rapid departure divested of his mantle: "'My knife is very sharp,' says one of the robbers, 'I sharpened it yesterday at the forge; I'll cut his throat in a flash.' And when the priest heard him he thought that he had been betrayed. He jumped down from the hill and fled all startled, but he left his mantle behind."[15]

"Du Vilain au buffet" presents a confusion that is essentially semantic rather than onomastic. Before a courtly assembly a brutal steward beats a peasant looking for a seat:

> — Je te presterai .I. seoir,"
> Ce dist li seneschaus par truffe;
> La paume hauce, une grant buffe
> Li done, puis fet .I. sifflet:
> "Or sié," fet il, "sor cest buffet
> Que je te preste, or te sié sus."
>
> (*Recueil*, III, 203)

"I'll lend you a seat," the steward said in jest. He raised his palm and gave him a great buffet, then whistled: "Now sit down," he said, "on this buffet that I lend you; go ahead, sit down."

The peasant, waiting until the end of the jongleurs' presentations, literally returns the loan and wins the prize for the best poetic performance:[16]

> Et dist li quens: "Il t'a rendu
> Ton buffet, et ce qu'ot du tien."
> Et dist li quens au vilain: "Tien
> Ma robe qui n'est pas usée,
> Quar fet as la meillor risée
> Seur toz les autres menestrels."
>
> (*Recueil*, III, 206)

And the count said: "He returned your buffet, and all he held of yours." Then the count said to the peasant: "Take my robe which is not worn out, for you have pulled off the best joke of all the minstrels."

What is significant here is not so much the double meaning of the word "buffet," but the fact that such word play is judged to be the essence of poetry. The peasant's jibe, in the specific context of poetic competition, succeeds where the other performers fail in disrobing the rich seigneur.

"Du Sot Chevalier" is the story of a knight so innocent of the world and its ways that he fails to consummate his marriage even at the end of a year. Desperate, his wife sends for her mother who offers him a lesson in the female anatomy and instructs him what to do:

> Si a ses cuisses descouvertes,
> Et puis a les jambes ouvertes,
> Se li monstra dant Connebert,
> Puis li a dit: "Sire Robert,
> Véez nul rien en cest val
> Ne contre mont, ne contre val?
> — Oïl, dame dist-il, .II. traus. . . .
> — Foutez le plus lonc anquenuit,
> Coment qu'il vous griet ne anuit. . . .

> Amis, le plus cort en batez,
> Quant vous an lonc vous combatez."
>
> *(Recueil,* I, 222–23)

She uncovered her thighs and opened her legs and showed him lady pussy. Then she said; "Sire Robert, do you see anything in this valley either up or downhill? — Yes, lady," he said, "two holes. . . . — Fuck the longer one tonight no matter what it costs you. . . . Friend, beat the short one (with your testicles) while doing combat with the longer."

That night a group of knights stranded in a storm send their squire to ask for shelter. The squire, hearing the husband repeat aloud his instructions ("Li plus lons ert foutuz, / Et li plus court sera batuz" [*Recueil,* I, 224]), reports that they have landed at the house of a pervert ("erite") who wants "to sodomize the tallest and beat the shortest." [17] "Du Sot Chevalier" is thus informed by the squire's misunderstanding of the referent of "short" and "long," as the rest of the tale revolves around the quid pro quo of the knights' attempts to avoid being sodomized and beaten.

Alongside the fabliaux in which dramatic interest is defined in terms of misunderstanding are those that indulge in some form of conscious wordplay, though the difference from the point of view of the reader seems more of degree than of kind. "De Pleine Bourse de sens," for example, is a story of adulterous deception that not only turns around the connection between poetry and dress, but whose equation of *robes* and *lobes* again betokens a fetishization of clothing emblematic of the tale: "Que li borjois une amie ot / Qu'il ama et vesti de robes, / Et cele le servoit de lobes" ("The burger had a mistress whom he loved and dressed in robes, but she dished out lies") (*Recueil,* III, 88). The unfaithful merchant, about to leave on business, asks his wife what dress—that is, what lie— she would like upon his return: "Volez vous guimple ne corroies, / Toissus d'or, aniaus, ou afiches?" (*Recueil,* III, 90). The wife's request for a "plaine borse de sen" sums up much of the problematic at hand. For the word *sen* can refer, first, to the notion of reasonableness or good sense (as in the jongleur d'Ely's "sen ou saver"); to return with a sack full of sense is to return chastened. But *sen* can also refer to "seed" from the Latin *semino* ("to beget," "engender," "bring forth," "procreate"); and to return with sacks or testicles full of seed is to return chaste, or to stop adulterous behavior. Finally, *sen* is a term employed in Old French to mean meaning itself, as in Chrétien de Troyes's distinction between "matière" and "sen"; and here the indicated reading has to do with bringing back the significance of the tale we read. There is, in other words, no way of separating theme—that of voyage, a straying from the marriage bed, and the purchase of cloth—from narrative structure. The fabliau is about the quest for meaning as well as for the proper mode of marital conduct.

"De Pleine Bourse de sens" is a tale which revolves around dress, reasonableness, and sense; and the tattered robe the merchant eventually buys for mistress and wife is an ill-fitting coat—"Achata li robe de pers / Mout par ot le sens à envers" (*Recueil*, III, 91)—that becomes the means to moral rectitude. Presented with it, the merchant's mistress sends him packing, and his wife demonstrates her love. The dress which he brings back, and which is indistinguishable from the fable the jongleur circulates, is a covering which, like the "mantel mautaillié," uncovers. What it uncovers is a representation of representation as ambiguity, the sign covering, or (in Macrobius's terms) the "interpretation" fitting, several and even discordant referents.[18] The robe is, finally, a "pleine bourse de sens"—a tale full of meanings—the author of which is the merchant who, transformed into a trouvère, discovers its sense ("Or avez vous trové le sen" [*Recueil*, III, 101]), which has precisely to do with the poetic potential of such wordplay: "Encore a on fabliau dou sen" (III, 102).

The example of "De Pleine Bourse de sens" is particularly compelling because it thematizes the capacity of language for multiple meaning, a certain fragmentation of linguistic sense, in terms of the specific body part whose loss signifies castration. It is not unique, however. "Boivin de Provins" includes among its multiple examples of multiple meaning a play upon the word "bourse." Having been seduced by a prostitute who intends to cut his purse, Boivins claims to have been castrated:

Ses braies monte; s'a veü
De sa borse les deux pendanz:
"Hai las!" fet il, "chetiz dolanz,
Tant ai hui fet male jornée!
Niece, ma borse m'est copée;
Ceste fame le m'a trenchie."

(*Recueil*, V, 61)

He lifts his pants; he saw the two straps of his purse:
"Alas," he said, "woe is me. I've had such a bad day!
Niece, my purse has been cut. This woman cut it off."

"De la Sorisete des estopes," the story of an unfaithful bride
who convinces her husband that she has left her genitals at her
mother's house, again links dismemberment to the dismemberment of meaning:

— Je voil," fait il, "vit avant traire:
Si vos fotra se j'onques puis,
Se vostre con delivre truis. . . .
— Mon con ne troveroiz vos pas.
— O est il donc? Nel me celez.
— Sire, qant savoir lo volez,
Jel vos dirai o est, par m'ame,
Muciez as piez do lit ma dame,
O jehui matin laissai. . . ."

(*Recueil*, IV, 159)

"I would like," he said, "to take my cock out. I will
screw you if I can and I can find your cunt. . . . — You
will not find my cunt. — Where is it then? Don't hide it
from me. — Sire, since you want to know I will tell you
where it is; by my soul it is at the foot of my mother's
bed, where I left it yesterday morning. . . ."

Thus, an imaginary—and purely verbal—castration is less the
sign of bodily mutilation than of a mutilation in language, of
language, around which "De la Sorisete des estopes" turns.
The tale combines a feigned separation of the body from its
"private part" with a separation of the "private part" from
its proper designation. And the elaborate wordplay upon the
common properties of the ragmouse and the female genitalia

(involving furriness, furtiveness, moisture) makes it increasingly clear that it is the cuckolded husband—and not his wife—who has been castrated.[19]

"De la Sorisete des estopes" is one of a series of fabliaux that articulates castration specifically in terms of a play on the word "con." "De Guillaume au faucon," to take another, is the story of a knight who so desires the wife of his lord that he refuses to eat. When asked by her husband the reason for Guillaume's conduct, the wife tries to hide behind what becomes—through the verbal ruse that seems autonomously to trap her—a self-indicting lie: "Sire, Guillaumes, que vez ci. / Si me requist vostre faucon, / Et ge ne l'en voil faire don" (*Recueil*, II, 111). The husband's granting of what seems like an innocent wish ("J'amasse mielz tuit li oisel . . . / Fussent mort que .I. jor entire / En eüst Guillaumes geü" [*Recueil*, II, 111]) implicates the double gift of bird and wife in the doubleness of language, as the "faucon" and the "faux con," or lying lady (with whom Guillaume would like to lie) become allied:

> Dist la Dame: "Or avez faucon;
> .II. besanz valent .I. mangon."
> Ce fu bien dit, .II. moz à un,
> Que il en auroit .II. por un,
> Et cil si ot ainz l'endemain
> Le faucon dont il ot tel faim,
> Et de la dame son deduit.
>
> (*Recueil*, II, 112)

The Lady said: "Now you have the falcon; two besants are worth one mangon." This was well put, two words for one. And he who desired the falcon so much had it the next day along with the pleasure of the lady.

Thus to the extent that language is cut off from univocal meaning, offering "two words for one," it serves to castrate the husband, to make him make himself a cuckold.

The doubling of value through the doubleness of language is best illustrated in "De Brunain la vache au prestre." A greedy priest, perverting or "doubling" the Parable of the Talents, reminds his congregation that "It is good to give, for

God who understands reason renders double to those who give willingly." [20] This initial linguistic ruse in which the temporal and spiritual are conflated leads to the ploy of a poor couple's gift of a meager beast that gives little milk and its eventual return leading the priest's fatted cow. Here again, the ambiguity is both economic and linguistic. For the cow which is doubled is in fact named Blère; "Doublère" and "deux Blères" are inescapable homonyms:

> "Ha, fet li vilains, bele suer,
> Voirement est Diex bon doublère,
> Quar li et autre revient Blère;
> Une grant vache amaine brune;
> Or en avons nous .II. por une."
>
> (*Recueil*, I, 134)

"Ha," said the peasant, "sweet sister, God is truly a generous doubler, for here comes Blère leading another big brown cow. Now we have two for one."

As the fabliau recalls, the cloak of stories is always lined; and beneath the ill-fitting garment of representation lies a *doublure*.

In a sense every fabliau that ends with a moral can be said to turn around the distance that the aphorism inscribes between the narrative and itself: e.g., "Tels cuide avancer qui recule" (*Recueil*, I, 48); "Mielz valt engiens que ne fait force" (III, 214); "Teus cuide cunchier autrui, / Qui tout avant cunchie lui (IV, 127); "Veritez est, et je le di, / Qu'amors vaint tout et tout vaincra / Tant com cis siecles durera" (V, 262); "Teus est de ces flabel la some; / Dahet feme qui despit home!" (VI, 116). Many tales, however, are also dramatic illustrations of proverbs. "De la Vielle qui oint la palme au chevalier," for example, is the story of an old woman who loses her two cows to a greedy provost. She consults a knight who advises her "to grease the provost's palm" and ends up by placing an actual piece of lard in his hand ("Lo lart par la paume li trait" [V, 158]). The dramatic interest of "De la Vielle" thus consists entirely of the doubling of literal and proverbial senses. So too "Le Plantez," the tale of a Norman who orders wine with his last penny, is dismayed when the tavern keeper spills it and is not reassured by his host's proverbial consolation "Ce est gaaigne qui te vient, / Car à celui qui vin espant / Vient, ce dit l'an, gaaigne grant" (III, 171). When the tavern keeper leaves to fetch something to eat the angry Norman opens the spigots of the barrels and, on reproach, offers similar solace: "Ne sez tu que tu me deïs / D'un po de vin que m'espendis, / Je gaaig-nerois à planté?" (III, 172). Finally, the tale known as "Le Sen-tier batu" offers the example of a fabliau informed by its aph-oristic beginning ("Folie est d'autrui ramprosner, / Ne gens de chose araisoner" [III, 247]), for this is the tale of a parlor game in which a woman mocks a man for his lack of beard. He, in turn, asks an indiscreet question ("Dame, respondez moi sanz guile; / A point de poil à vo poinille?); and when she answers in the negative ("Sachiez qu'il n'en y a point"), he venges himself with the proverbial "en sentier / Qui est batus ne croist point d'erbe" (III, 248). For Jean de Condé, in other words, it is not a question even of castration; a little shaving of the genitals suffices to sustain the mutual implication of se-mantic doubling and dismemberment.

At an extreme, the linguistic play that is so basic to the fabliaux eliminates the question of meaning altogether or re-duces words to a pure phenomenon of sound. "De l'Escui-ruel," for instance, presents a rebellious daughter forbidden "to name the thing which hangs between the legs of men" yet so intrigued by the interdiction that she repeats it obses-sively.[21] The beginning of this tale of displaced meanings be-comes a masculine equivalent of the "Dit des cons":

> "Vit," dist ele, "Dieu merci, vit!
> Vit dirai je, cui qu'il anuit,
> Vit, chetive! vit dist mon pere,
> Vit dist ma suer, vit dist mon frere,
> Et vit dit nostre chamberiere,
> Et vit avant et vit arriere
> Nomme chascuns à son voloir."[22]

"Prick," she said, "Thank God, prick! I will say prick no matter who it harms, prick, little wretch. Prick says my father, prick says my sister, prick says my brother, and prick says our chambermaid; and prick up front and prick in back. Everyone can say it as much as he likes."

In a passage reminiscent of "Les .IIII. Souhaits Saint Martin" and in which the entire body becomes a mass of sexual organs, "De l'Escuiruel" transforms meaning into sound, while at the same time it thematizes castration.

If fabliaux like "De l'Escuiruel," "Des .IIII. Souhaits," or "Du Sot Chevalier" for that matter, seem to function according to a certain verbal automatism—a play of the signifier divested of referent—other tales produce similar effects through linguistic confusion and bilingualism. "Du Prestre qui dist la passion," for example, contains the story of a "silly and crazy priest" who one Good Friday so jumbles the pages of the service that he appears to hallucinate in Latin:[23]

> Que li prestres lor commença
> Et prist à dire isnelepas,
> Primes en halt puis en bas:
> "*Dixit Dominus Domino meo. . . .*"
> Lors prist à crier: "Barraban! . . ."
> Et li prestres, qui toute voie
> Lisoit le cors de son sautier,
> Reprent hautement à crier,
> Et dit: "*Crucifige eum! . . .*"
> *Mais au clerc ennuia forment,*
> *Et dist au prestre: "Fac finis!"*
> Et il li dist: "*Non fac*, amis
> *Usque ad mirabilia.*"
>
> (*Recueil*, V, 81–82)

The priest then began and started to say on the spot, first out loud then to himself: "*Dixit Dominus Domino meo. . . .*" Then he began to cry: "*Barraban! . . .*" And the priest who was reading the body of his psalter began to cry out and said: "*Crucifige eum! . . .*" But this annoyed a clerk who said to the priest: "*Fac finis!*" And he replied: "*Non fac*, friend, *usque ad mirabilia.*"

The author of "Du Prestre qui dist la passion" recognizes, moreover, that the priest's confusion is synonymous with his own:

> "*Dixit Dominus Domino meo.*"
> Mais ge ne vos puis pas en *o*
> Trover ici conçonancie;
> Si est bien droiz que ge vos die
> Tot le mielz que ge porrai metre.
>
> (*Recueil*, V, 81)

"*Dixit Dominus Domino meo.*" But I cannot for the life of me find here a rhyme with *o*. It is only right that I tell you as best I can.

The "jumbled pages" of the service are, in other words, those of the jongleur; and the split that the alternation between Old French and Latin introduces to the text is inseparable from the difference between madness and reason responsible for the tale's comic effect, or the distance that writing inscribes between the poet and itself.

The way in which the narrator reproduces the movement of that which he narrates underscores a doubleness at the core of "Du Prestre qui dit la passion." In this it is not unique; poems containing more than one tongue—limit cases of the Otherness of the literary text—constitute a virtual subgenre of the fabliaux. "De Deux Angloys et de l'anel," for example, turns around the attempt to reproduce certain English words phonetically in Old French as well as around the semantic confusions which such an attempt engenders. Thus one Englishman, sick and having slept fitfully, asks in a mixture of English and French for lamb ("Se tu avez .I. anel cras / Mi porra bien mengier, ce croi" [*Recueil*, II, 179]); his companion, having misunderstood, serves him a castrated ass instead:

> "Quel beste m'as tu ci porté?
> — Anel," fait il, "en charité.
> — Anel?" fait il, "par seint Almon,
> Cestui n'est mie filz moton?
> — Si est, pour ane ge chatai,
> Tot de plus grant que ge gardai."
>
> (*Recueil*, II, 181)

— What animal have you brought here? — Lamb," he said, "by charity. — Lamb?," he said, "by Saint Almon, this is no son of a sheep? — It is, because of the ass I castrated which was the largest I could find."

The confusion between the two understandings of the word "anel" reduces both interlocutors to animal sounds:

> Cestui n'est mie fils *bèhè*.
> Quoi dites vos, Alein, que est?
> Ce ne fu mie fielz berbis.
> — Tu dites voir, par seint Felix.
> Foi que ge doi à seint Joban,
> Cestui fu filz *ihan, ihan* . . .
>
> (*Recueil*, II, 181)

This is no son of *bah-bah*. What are you saying, Alan, what is it? This is no son of a lamb. — You are right, by Saint Felix. By the faith I owe Saint Joban, this is a son of *hee-haw*.

If the two Englishmen are turned into beasts (*bestournés*), it is because language itself has been denatured. And the castration of the ass becomes the equivalent of butchering a foreign tongue; the cutting of a suffix serves as a reminder of the naturalness with which speech is betrayed: "Son bon li velt dire en françois, / Mais la langue torne à englois / Que ce ne fu mie merveille." [24]

In its stretching of Old French to the point at which, under the phonetic system of English, it becomes unintelligible "De Deux Anglois et de l'anel" points toward those tales where dramatic interest and comic effect are based on the juxtaposition of more than one tongue. "Du Prestre qui fu mis au lardier," the story of a concupiscent priest's imprisonment in a meat locker, offers the example of a fabliau where mixed metrical form is doubled by the bilingualism of the prisoner's attempt to escape by communicating with a brother:

> "*Frater, pro Deo*
> *Me delibera;*
> *Reddam tam cito*
> Ce qu'il coustera."
> Quant l'oy, en haut s'escria:

> "Çavetiers me doivent amer de cuer fin
> Quant à mon lardier fais parler latin."
>
> (*Recueil*, II, 29)

"*Frater, pro Deo / Me delibera; / Reddam tam cito* no matter
what it costs." When he heard it he cried out loud:
"Cobblers should love me dearly since I know how to
make my meat locker speak Latin."

Further, the motif of the inanimate object that speaks suggests
an interpretation of "Du Prestre qui fu mis au lardier" based
upon the project of poetry itself. If the cobbler's initial delight
at the ventriloquism of his meat locker is motivated by the de-
sire for gain ("Esgar, mon lardier a latin parlé; / Vendre le
vouloie" [*Recueil*, II, 27]), the final exchange of speech for
money turns him into a poet: "Le Prestre n'osa / Le mot re-
fuser; / A Baillet ala / Vint livres conter" (II, 29).

The mixture of Old French and Latin is most evident in the
series of short pieces published by Méon/Barbazan for which
classification as fabliaux remains problematic. "Des Fames,
des dez et de la taverne," for example, is more on the order of
a *dit* akin to the *griesches* of Rutebeuf or, proleptically, to Vil-
lon's tavern songs:

> Je maine bone vie *semper quum possum*
> Li Taverniers m'apele, je di, *ecce assum;*
> A despendre le mien *semper paratus sum,*
> Cant je pens en mon cuer et *meditatus sum*:
> *Ergo dives habet nummos, sed non habet ipsum.*[25]

I lead a good life *semper quum possum*. The tavern keeper
calls me, and I say, *ecce assum*; to spend my money *semper
paratus sum*, when I think in my heart and *meditatus sum*:
Ergo dives habet nummos, sed non habet ipsum.

The Old French and Latin of "Des Fames, des dez et de la ta-
verne" seem to complement each other; they form a continu-
ous discourse despite the obvious difference of tongue. A se-
ries of bilingual prayers, on the other hand, accentuate an
internal tension that is at once structural and thematic. Each is
organized according to a Latin rendering of the Lord's Prayer

or the Credo interrupted by a train of the poet's thought that could not be further from the efficacy of divine grace.[26] The "Patenostre d'amours" is, in this respect, particularly interesting:

> *Pater noster.* Diex pour m'amie
> Qui m'a mis en si dure vie
> Que je ne puis à li parler,
> He? Diex qui m'i porra aler,
> Et dire li que je li mant
> Que je sui son léal amant.
> *Qui es in coelis.* A grant paine
> Me tieng un jor en la semaine
> De li véoir ou tempre, ou tart. . . .
> *Sanctificetur.* Douce Dame
> Qui est sauveresse de m'ame. . . .
> *Nomen tuum.* Veraiement
> M'est vis qu'ele est apertement
> La plus bele. . . .
> *Adveniat.* Diex, que ferai?
> Por sa grant biauté morrai,
> Je le sai bien. *Regnum tuum.*
> Vers li n'ai pas le cuer felon.
> *Fiat. . . .*[27]

Pater noster. God, for my love who makes me suffer so since I can't speak to her. Ha? God, who can go to tell her that I send her the message that I am her loyal lover? *Qui es in coelis.* With great effort I manage to see her one day a week early or late. . . . *Sanctificetur.* Sweet lady who is the savior of my soul. . . . *Nomen tuum.* Truly it is my opinion that she is clearly the most beautiful. . . . *Adveniat.* God, what will I do? For her great beauty I will die, I know it well. *Regnum tuum.* I have a pure heart with respect to her. *Fiat. . . .*

Not only does the "Patenostre d'amours" contain two languages, but the discourse that each implies—of liturgy and of the courtly lyric—are so inimical as to constitute a limit case of linguistic doubling. One with significance, moreover, for our understanding of the fabliaux. The language of sexual longing forms a background to the intrusive elements of prayer and radically poses the question of relation between desire and the verbal schism that reaches an extreme in the bilingual poem.

What is the relation between the poet's desire for his lady—the Other—and the Otherness of the Latin prayer that seems to stand as its repression? To what degree is the doubleness of the text a function of the poet's desire? Desire a function of the duplicity of the text? What is the relation of a bifurcated poem like the "Patenostre d'amours" to the representations of the fragmented body with which we began the present discussion?

There is, first of all, no denying within the fabliaux a current of literalism that attributes castration to sexual desire. As in the story of Abelard, mutilation is the direct result of transgression and transgression the proper of the priest. What is less evident perhaps is the essentially anecdotal status of such a causal relation compared to its corollary. For if dismemberment of the body, as we have seen, is linked to the dismemberment of meaning, then the dismemberment of meaning becomes the source of sexual desire, as in the myth of the birth of Venus around Saturn's disjected member. The linguistic gaps, or differences, of which the bilingual poem contains the most extreme examples, are the source of the theme of erotic longing and not the inverse. The language which covers—and always covers imperfectly—does not stand in specular relation to the body (or to any body of representation), but on the contrary, seems even to engender that of which it speaks. This is the point of the series of fabliaux concerned (again like the *Roman de la rose*) with the naming of sexual organs.

"Sweet friend," says the wife to her husband in "De Porcelet," "let's give a name to your little thing ('à vostre rien') and to my cunt ('à mon con'). . . . Let my cunt be called piglet ('porcelet') because it is never clean; and your thing, I don't know—oh, let's call it wheat ('fromant') since that's a nice name."[28] Such a focusing upon the partial object, which we have identified with castration, implies a loss of univo-

cal meaning. Indeed, "De Porcelet" turns around a series of
ambiguities having to do with food, ingestion, excretion, and
meaning:

> Li vallez lait aler .I. pet
> El giron à la damoisele:
> "Que est ce or, sire?" fait ele;
> "Qu'avez vos fait en mon devant?
> — Dame, ce est brans qui espant,
> Por doner à vostre porcel,
> Que foi que je doit saint Marcel,
> Do froment, qui est en despans,
> N'i est remis for que li brans.
> — Commant, sire, est donques failliz
> Li fromans? Donc est malbailliz
> Porcelet, se Deus me doint sen,
> Qu'il n'a cure de vostre bran."
>
> (*Recueil*, IV, 145)

The man broke wind into the woman's lap. "What's this,
sir?" she asked. "What have you done to my front?
— Lady, this is bran that escapes, to give to your piglet,
because, by the faith I owe Saint Marcel, of the wheat
I've been dosing out only the bran is left. — How's that,
sir, is the wheat all gone? My little piglet will be upset, if
God gives me sense, for he doesn't care for your bran."

"De Porcelet" thus articulates a process of pejoration by which
food is turned to excrement; wheat to bran (or in French, *son*);
and meaning (*sens*) to sound.

In "De Porcelet" desire is the product of an act of naming
since the fabliau recounts the story of a marriage whose erotic
edges have been rounded by habit and which, because of a re-
viving imposition of names and its narrative elaboration, ends
with the insatiability of women: "Qant plus manjue, plus fain
a; / Fous fu qui primes les troua." ("The more it ate, the hun-
grier it got; he was crazy who split them in the first place"
(*Recueil*, IV, 146). "The one who split them in the first place"
is, of course, the one who first introduced difference through
names, or the trouvère himself. Like the weary husband, the
performer exhausts—through repetition or through writing—

the presence of his own performance or voice. And the husband's warning to his wife might also apply to the jongleur and his public: "Vostre merci, laissiez m'an paiz, / Que tant ai fait vos volantez / Que toz me sui desfromantez" (*Recueil*, I, 146).

A version of "De Porcelet" is to be found in "C'est de la Dame qui aveine demandoit pour Morel sa provende avoir." Here again, an initial state of desire ("Par amistiez et par delit, / Jà ne queissent issir du lit" [*Recueil*, I, 319]) vanquished by habit ("Orent entr'aus .II. establie, / Si vos dirai la mencolie" [I, 320]) is revived by an imperious husband's act of linguistic deflection:

> Toutes foiz qu'avec moi seras,
> Soit en lit ou en autre place,
> Et tu vourras que je te face
> Se jolif mestier amoureux:
> Se me diras: "Biax frère doux,
> Faites Moriax ait de l'avainne."
>
> (*Recueil*, I, 320)

Each time you're with me, whether in bed or anywhere else, and you want me to do the sweet deed of love, say to me: "Sweet brother, make sure Morel has his oats."

Again, this renders his wife insatiable:

> Cilz s'aparoille et monte sus
> Qu'amont, qu'aval, que sus que jus;
> Ainsis fist à pou de sejour
> Dès le couchier jusques au jour.
>
> (*Recueil*, I, 324)

This one got ready and mounted up, up and down, on the bottom and on top. For a while she was doing it from dusk to dawn.

Finally exhausted ("Frailles, vuis et touz espichiez" [*Recueil*, I, 326]), the husband of "C'est de la Dame" adopts a tactic identical to that of the husband of "De Porcelet" ("Son cul torna en son giron, / Et li chia tout environ / Que bran, que merde, qu'autre choze" [I, 328]). Thus the transformation of bodily function into the equivalent of a poetic act—the cloaking of coitus behind cloaca—is the source of desire that, transformed into reflex, is evacuated. As in the examples of "Jouglet" and "De Audigier," the tale itself becomes—through repetition— dead, fecal, recycled matter.

"De l'Escuiruel," which contains an example of verbal automatism attached specifically to the detached phallus, is particularly interesting in light of the problem at hand. For the young girl fascinated by the proper word for the penis ("Et vit avant et vit arriere / Nomme chascuns à son voloir" [*Recueil*, V, 103]) is not aroused by naming it, or even by seeing it, but by its improper designation as a squirrel:

> "Ha! Robert! Dieu vous beneïe!
> Dites moi, se Dieu vous aït,
> Que vous tenez;" et il li dist:
> "Dame, ce est .I. escuiruel;
> Volez le vous? — Oïl, mon vuel,
> Aus mains le tenisse je ore!"
>
> (*Recueil*, V, 104)

"Ha! Robert! God bless you! Tell me, so help you God, what you have there." And he said, "Lady, this is a squirrel; do you want it? — Yes, I would like to hold it in my hands!"

The phallus/squirrel is the first in a series of similarly false designations. Robert's testicles become a nest ("Ele avoit la coille veüe: / 'Robin,' fet ele, 'qu'est ce ici? / — Bele,' fet il, 'ce est son ni'" [*Recueil*, V, 105]); the testes, an egg ("'— Voire,' fet el, 'je sent .I. oef.'" [V, 105]); orgasm, vomiting ("Et a vouchié et a vomi" [V, 107]); and semen, egg white ("L'aubun m'en cort par mi les nages!" [V, 107]). This set of verbal improprieties, taken as a whole, informs the narrative of "De l'Escuiruel," the story of a seduction and loss of virginity:

> Par cest fablel vueil enseignier
> Que tels cuide bien chastier
> Sa fille de dire folie,
> Et quant plus onques le chastie,

Tant le met l'en plus en la voie
De mal fere, se Dieus me voie.

Explicit de l'Escuiruel (Recueil, V, 108)

By this fabliau I want to show that some people think
they are warning their daughter against speaking fool-
ishly; but the more they warn them, the more they put
them on the way to doing evil, so help me God.

To our initial question concerning the origin of desire, the re-
sponse can only be something on the order of language or, as
the poet makes clear in the above *explicit*, the fabliau itself.

What "De L'Escuiruel," "C'est de la Dame," and "De Por-
celet" transmit is not so much the narrative account of the
sexual act as an account of sexuality that is indissociable from
narrative. It is the representation of the body, and more pre-
cisely the deflection of the proper transformed into story, that
constitutes the eroticism of the fabliaux. This may seem like
an excessive claim, but one sustained nonetheless by the
works dealing with the naming of sexual organs. And by
those that prohibit their naming as well. "De la Pucelle qui
abreva le polain," for instance, begins with an interdiction of
the proper ("Ne voloit oïr la pucele / De foutre à nul fuer"
[*Recueil*, IV, 199]) as does the tale whose title, in the phrase of
Alexandre Leupin, contains an "entire poetic project"—"De
la Damoisele qui n'ot parler de fotre qui n'aüst mal au cuer." [29]
This is the story of a farmer unable to keep hired laborers who
speak too explicitly of sex to his daughter "who cannot stand
to listen to a steward speak of lechery, of prick or balls or
anything else," for she becomes "sick to her stomach" at
such talk. [30]

What the father of "De la Damoisele" fails to understand,
however, is that the deflection of the proper—the words "vit,"
"coilles," and "foutre"—does not upset his daughter, but ex-
cites her. The clever David who, like the poet, "understood
ruse and guile" ("Qui mout savoit barat et guile" [*Recueil*, V,
25]), knows in particular how to make the body speak:

Et Daviez sa main avale
Droit au pertuis desoz lo vantre. . . .

Bien taste tot o la main destre,
Puis demande que ce puet estre.
"Par foi," fet ele, "c'est mes prez. . . .
— Et que est ce en mi cest pré
C'est fosse soéve et plaine?
— Ce est," fait ele, "ma fontaine. . . .
— Et que est ce ici après,"
Fet Daviez, "en ceste engarde?
— C'est li corneres qui la garde."

(*Recueil*, V, 28–29)

And David lowered his hand right down to the hole be-
low the belly. . . . He felt it up with his right hand, then
asked what it could be. "By faith," she said, "it is my
meadow. . . . — And what's this in the middle of the
meadow, this soft and wide opening? — It is," she said,
"my fountain. . . . — And what's this here behind," he
asked, "in this enclosure? — It is the trumpeter that
guards it."

If the maiden who cannot tolerate direct talk of bodily parts
seems only too anxious to speak of "meadow," "fountain,"
and "trumpeter," so too is David cognizant of the erotic power
of deflected speech:

Tantost sor lui sa main remet . . .
Tant qu'el l'a par lo vit saisi,
Et demande: "Que est ici,
Daviet, si roide et dur,
Que bien devroit percer .I. mur?
— Dame," fait il, "c'est mes polains. . . ."
Les .II. coillons taste et remue:
"Sire," demande, "Daviet,
Que est or ce, en ce sachet?"
Fait ele, "sont ce .II. luisiaus?"
Davis fu de respondre isniaus:
"Dame, ce sont dui mareschal
Qui ont à garder mon cheval."

(*Recueil*, V, 30)

Then she put her hand on him. . . . So much so that she
grabbed him by the cock and asked: "What is this,

David, so hard and thick that it could pierce a wall?
— Lady," he said, "this is my steed. . . ." She felt the
two balls: "Sir David," she asked, "what do we have here
in this sack? Are they two balls?" David was quick to re-
spond: "Lady, these are two marshals whose duty it is to
guard my horse."

Again, desire originates neither in contact with the body nor
in the proper designation of bodily parts, but in the deflection
of the proper that becomes—in "De la Damoisele," as in this
entire series of tales—the equivalent of narrative: "'Davi, met
lou en mon pré pestre, / Ton biau polain, se Deus te gart.'"[31]
Naming comes in the fabliaux to constitute the space of nar-
rative, and the space of narrative that of desire.

This may seem like a minor point, one based, after all, on
a group of idiosyncratic examples. Yet the explicitness with
with "De Porcelet," "C'est de la Dame," "De l'Escuiruel,"
"De la Pucelle," and "De la Damoisele" treat the relation be-
tween definition, narrative, and desire makes them central to
our understanding of sexuality within the genre as a whole.
This is especially true given that the most acknowledged re-
cent attempts to deal with the comic tale have focused upon
the issue of linguistic property.[32] Nykrog, for example, claims
to have examined the genre with "une objectivité toute médi-
cale" (FN, p. 209); and the fact that, according to Nykrog,
one finds the unqualified use of the verb "foutre" only seven
times, added to the infrequency of the nouns "vit," "con,"
and "couilles," stands as proof of the fabliaux's essentially
courtly nature: "On constate que des périphrases courtoises,
ou au moins fort décents, y sont employées bien plus fré-
quemment que les expressions moins voilées" (FN, p. 209).[33]
For Ménard, the reluctance of the medieval poet to speak di-
rectly of the sexual act reveals not only "the medieval couple's
discomfort at naming coitus" (FM, p. 149), but betrays the
author's "good taste" as well (FM, p. 147). The question of
linguistic deflection is then a matter of style, of "sensibility"
(FM, p. 163), and of social distinction: "Si l'on aspire à une
certaine distinction, on ne parle pas en public de choses qui relè-
vent du sexe et de la scatologie" (FM, p. 145). Ménard main-
tains, to return to the example at hand, that "De la Damoi-

sele" is about the limits of polite conversation: "Le conte de la 'damoisele qui n'ot parler de foutre qui n'aüst mal au cuer' exprime à sa manière que pour la politesse mondaine le mot *foutre* est prohibé" (FM, p. 154).

Ménard's concern with "bienséances" coupled with Nykrog's squeamishness ("Le lecteur m'excusera de ne pas les citer; je préfère me borner à donner la référence" [FN, p. 212]) resemble more than a little the "maiden who could not hear talk of fucking without becoming sick to her stomach." But however ironic the critic's modesty may be, it renders urgent what I have maintained all along—that the erotic interest of the fabliaux consists neither of anything like a natural act (a naturalism of the body) nor of the use of direct speech to describe such an act (a naturalism of language), but of the refusal of the proper that characterizes the tales analyzed above: a denaturing. Indeed, if there is any pleasure attached to sex in the Old French comic tale (and the question of "if" is worth posing), such pleasure derives less from the body than from a deferral in speech, of speech, that substitutes for the object or act.

This is not to deny either the reality or the importance of the all too obvious obsession with sexual organs. Such a fixation is virtually indistinguishable from the theme of castration writ so large across the genre as a whole. What I am suggesting, on the other hand, is that the narrative fixation upon the partial object is at the origin of sexual desire within the comic tale and not the reverse. The preoccupation with sexual members is at once the product of and a fascination with narrative and not its referent. Narrative is the catalyst of desire and not its simple reflection or representation, as per the traditional view of the fabliaux as "natural texts," "texts without literary artifice," pure manifestations of "l'esprit gaulois."

The fundamentally "literary" origin of the body's pleasure is the point of the series of tales involving the displacement of direct speech toward indirect expression and, ultimately, narrative elaboration—"De Porcelet," "De l'Escuiruel," "C'est de la Dame," "De la Damoisele," "De la Pucele qui abevra le polain," but also "De la Pucelle qui vouloit voler" (*Recueil*, IV, 208). These are parables of desire which insist that desire originates in parables. The theme of arousal as a result of the invention of stories within the story we read is, in fact, a corollary of such a paradigm and can be found throughout the fabliaux. In "Du Fevre de Creeil," for example, it is the husband's description of his apprentice's member, and not the organ itself or his wife's libido, that creates her desire for it:

> "Dame," fet il, "se Diex m'aït,
> Je ne vi onques si grant membre,
> Que je sache ne que moi membre,
> Come a Gautiers nostre serjanz;
> Quar, se ce fust uns granz jaianz,
> Si en a-il assés par droit;
> Merveille est quant il est à roit;
> Je le vos di tout sanz falose.
> — Quar parlez à moi d'autre chose,"
> Fet cele, cui semble qu'el hée
> Ce dont ele est si enbrasée . . .
> (*Recueil*, I, 233)

"Lady," he said, "so help me God, I never saw such a big tool as that of Gautiers our apprentice; for even if he were a giant, he would have more than enough. It is a marvel when it is stiff, I can tell you without exaggerating. — Speak about something else," said the one who pretended to hate that which she was burning for.

The sadistic blacksmith, jealous of Gautiers and anxious to cut his organ off, is in reality an inscription of the poet who, from the point of view of a third party, does to his audience what the forger of the tale does to his wife. Thus this tale of dismemberment, desire, and the desire for dismemberment originates in a prior act of castration synonymous with narrative itself.

A narrative fixation upon the partial at once engenders desire and the desire for narrative. This defining tautology is repeated in the fabliaux over and over again; and it is nowhere more evident than in the tales of the three women who find alternately a phallus and a ring. In "Des .III. Dames qui trouverent un vit" the desire for rhyme with which the tale begins is linked to the desire for the found object:

Mais s'il i a consonancie,
Il ne m'en chaut qui mal en die,
Car ne puet pas plaisir à touz
Consonancie sanz bons moz;
Or les oiez teus comme il sont.
　　Trois dames aloient au Mont,
Mès je ne sai de quel païs;
Puis oï conter, ce m'est vis,
Que .II. coiz et .I. vit mout gros
Troverent, ou il n'ot point d'os.
Icele qui aloit devant
Le prist et muça maintenant,
Quar bien savoit que ce estoit;
Mès l'autre qui après venoit
Dit qu'ele en avroit sa part.

(*Recueil*, V, 32)

But as long as there is rhyme, I do not mind who criti-
cizes it, for rhyme without clever turns of phrase cannot
please. Now listen to them.

Three ladies went up a hill, but I don't know in what
country. Then I heard tell, it seems to me, that they
found an enormous penis and two balls. The one walk-
ing ahead took it and shook it for she knew what it was;
but the one who came after said she wanted her part.

The three ladies who find ("trouverent") a phallus remain in-
distinguishable from the trouvère who composes rhyme, just
as the quarrel over who will keep that which they all desire
becomes synonymous with poetic composition. The one who
invents the best story within the story of "Des .III. Dames"
will get to keep the prize, as the abbess, mistress of invention,
convinces them that the phallus is the door-knocker recently
stolen from the front door: "C'est le toraill de nostre porte /
Qui l'autre jor fu adiré" (*Recueil*, V, 35). Thus the tale of the
partial object par excellence, detached and circulating like the
dead priest of the tales of "De la longue Nuit" in search of
meaning, ends in the narrative invention of its own origin.

As in "Des .III. Dames qui trouverent un vit," the found
ring of "Des .III. Dames qui trouverent l'anel" represents a

fixation linked to the desire for the phallus, or in this case, for a story: "Among them they swore by Jesus that the one who could best deceive her husband in order to do her will with her lover would have the ring, and it would be hers."[34] Hence what is thematized as a competition based upon inventiveness, and which mirrors the rivalry of jongleurs in "Des Deux Bordeurs ribauz" and "La Contregengle," spawns three narratives of castration and deceit.

The first lady tonsures her drunk husband's head and deposits him in front of the entrance to an abbey; he is convinced, upon awakening, that God has called him to the priesthood. The second leaves home to cook some eels and doesn't return for a week; when she does she convinces her gullible husband that she has been absent for only a few hours. The third inventive woman disguises herself such that her husband ends up marrying her to her lover. In each case the deception that is staged by the three makers of tales within the tale becomes indistinguishable from the fabliau itself. "Les .III. Dames qui trouverent un anel" comes to mean literally "the three women who found a ring" and "the three women who composed—in the medieval sense of *trobar* (trouvère, troubadour)—the poem." The ring, in turn, represents merely an empty center from which the fabliau, as a parable of desire demonstrating the desire for fable, is generated.

Far from the plenitude of what is taken for a certain naturalism of the body and according to which "les appétits charnels sont présents partout" (FM, p. 122), the fabliaux are narratives of absence which stage their own genesis more explicitly than any other medieval form. "Les .III. Dames" is in this respect a good example of such staging in which decor, timing, and disguise, along with the invention of fables, combine to transform the three protagonists and generators of their own story into an inscription of the poet within the tale. To the degree that the comic story in fact contains inventors of fictions within fiction, it uncovers the underpinnings of its own self-contained creation. It exposes the ruse of poetry which is precisely, as I have emphasized from the beginning, the refusal to specify an origin or a destination outside of the text. In its resistance to univocal meaning, the fabliau is even capable of incorporating the ultimate ruse—which is the de-nunciation of ruses. "Folie est d'autrui ramprosner, / Ne gens de chose araisoner," asserts Jean de Condé in "Le Sentier batu," a fable which in its triumphant wittiness contradicts its opening injunction (*Recueil*, III, 247).

Just as "Les .III. Dames qui trouverent un anel" turns around the invention of narratives within the narrative, and thus permits us to identify its heroines with a hypothetical au-thor, so too in "Les .III. Avugles de Compiengne" the explicit identification of the poet ("Cortebarbe a cest fablel fet" [*Re-cueil*, I, 70]) is overshadowed by the role of the cleric who sets into motion an elaborate scenario of deceit. The wander-ing scholar first pretends to offer a coin to three blind men who proceed to spend it drinking. They discover the truth only when asked to pay; but the cleric, meanwhile, manages through another clever trick to displace the debt upon the lo-cal parish priest who eventually convinces the tavern keeper that he is mad.

"Les .III. Avugles" reveals a desire for narrative that is thematized throughout. The cleric's love of deceit ("Li clers esraument se porvoit, / Qui les veut falordant" [*Recueil*, I, 71]) and the blind men's wish to believe ("Chascuns cuide que ses compains l'ait" [I, 71]) mirror the public's wish for the salu-tary effects of fable: "Fablel sont bon a escouter: / Maint duel, maint mal font mesconter / Et maint anui et maint meffet" (I, 70). The fable itself seems to spring from nowhere. It origi-nates spontaneously—by a chance encounter along the road to Senlis—in the invented gesture of a false gift. Nor can such an open economy of narration, producing as it does a tale with-out source, be separated from the open economy of expen-diture that "Les .III. Avugles" entails. For the coin, like the text, is the object of pure speculation. It motivates the ex-change of words for the belief (or credit) first of the blind men, then of the tavern keeper, and finally of the parish priest. In this it is paradigmatic of the tale—originless, ambulatory, unlocatable:

> "Liquels l'a. Be! je n'en ai mie.
> — Dont l'a Robers Barbe-florie?

— Non ai, mès vous l'avez, bien sai.
— Par le cuer bieu, mie n'en ai.
— Li quels l'a dont?— Tu l'as.— Mès tu."

(Recueil, I, 75)

"Which one has it. Bah! I don't have it at all. — Then
does Robert Barbefleurie have it? — I don't have it, but I
know that you have it. — By the heart of God, I don't.
— Who has it then? — You have it. — No, you."

The unsubstantial coin reflects then the unstable position of
the inscribed author who is at once an observer of and an
agent in the tale he sets in motion: "Et li clers tout adès de-
meure, / Por ce qu'il veut savoir lor fin." ("And the cleric re-
mained there because he wanted to know their end" [I, 74].)

The fabliaux that stage their own genesis are so numerous
that the few I have selected for discussion are merely repre-
sentative of a principle of functionalism—the exposure of
the architectonic underpinnings of poetic creation—operative
within the genre as a whole. "Du Chevalier qui fist sa fame
confesse," to take another example, is the story of a knight's
desire for a tale; or to be more specific, for the story of his
wife's tail: "En leu de moine à li vendrai, / Et sa confession
orrai."[35] The darkness of the room, the disguise of the voice,
the change of clothing ("Et quant fu nuis les dras vestit; / Il
chanja trestout son abit") do elicit the unexpected revelation
that his dying wife has also been unfaithful—"Més moult
mauvèse fame estoie, / Quar à mes garçons me livorie, / Et
avoeques moi les couchoie."[36] Confronted, the wife claims to
have recognized her husband whom she punished with lies:
"Se dame Diex mon cors garisse, / Bien vous reconnui au par-
ler" (Recueil, I, 187). What the husband seeks, in essence, is to
know the truth of his wife's sexual organs or, as in the series
of fabliaux discussed below, to make her vagina speak. The
elaborate staging of confession is complicated, however, by
the impossibility of determining the living truth of the dying
woman's invention. For if the knight in the beginning repre-
sents an inscription of the poet, his role as stager is usurped by
the wife whose clever reading of the situation transforms her
curious husband (who desires the story of his wife's sexual

organ more than the organ itself) into a frustrated reader of the narrative he originally spawns. At the center, the unknowable gap—the "trou" of the "trouvère"—stands inviolable, as the poet, like the (guilty?) woman, remains undefined.

Among the fabliaux that stage their own production none is more significant than "De Boivin de Provins." Here the poet recounts the tale of a trickster who stations himself on the front steps of a brothel and begins to recite the story of his riches and lost family. Overhearing what seems like a ready opportunity for gain, the whores and pimps decide to divest Boivin of his wealth. They dispatch Mabile, the madam, who pretends to be his long-lost niece. After a copious meal for which he offers somewhat gratuitously to pay, she sends him to bed with a supposed virgin, Ysane, whom she has instructed to cut his purse strings. But Boivin has beaten her to it; and once he has had his will of her, he disappears. In his absence the whores and pimps quarrel, like the blind men of "Les .III. Avugles," over who really has the purse and who has tricked whom. Meanwhile, Boivin has withdrawn to the local chief of police's house to tell his tale of adventure in exchange for food and money.

The assimilation of the hero and the poet is evident from the beginning. What does Boivin want but to be spoken of? "A la foire voudra aler, / Et si fera de lui parler" (*Recueil*, V, 52). The means to be spoken of are, further, the very means of poetic invention with all the trappings of dramatic performance: make-up, props, and costume. Boivin dons the ill-fitting coats of theatrical representation:

> Vestuz se fu d'un burel gris,
> Cote, et sorcot, et chape ensamble,
> Qui tout fu d'un, si com moi samble;
> Et si ot coiffe de borras;
> Ses sollers ne sont mis à las,
> Ainz sont de vache dur et fort;
> Et cil, qui mout de barat sot,
> .I. mois et plus estoit remese
> Sa barbe qu'ele ne fu rese;
> .I. aguillon prist en sa main,

> Por ce que mieus samblast vilain:
> Une borse grant acheta,
> .XII. deniers dedenz mis a . . .
>
> (*Recueil*, V, 52)

He dressed himself in a grey rough cloth, his coat, over-
coat, and hat which were all of a piece it seems to me.
And he had a hood of hemp cloth. His shoes were not
laced but were made of tough cowhide. And this one,
who knew a lot of tricks, let his beard go for a month
without shaving. He took a stick in his hand in order to
look like a peasant. He bought a great big purse and put
12 deniers in it . . .

As if he were following stage directions, Boivin positions
himself in front of the brothel ("Iluec s'assist desus .I. fust; /
Delez lui mist son aguillon, / .I. poi torna son dos vers l'uis"
[*Recueil*, V, 53]) where he invents both himself and his for-
tune: "By faith," he says, "now that I am far from the fair and
in a safe place far from people I can count my money all alone.
This is what smart people do. Let's see: I had from Roger 39
sous; 12 deniers were kept by Giraud who helped me sell my
two oxen. Let him hang for keeping them! . . . I had 19 sous
from Sorin. I was not false with these ones, for my friend
Gautiers didn't give me so many deniers as I had at the least;
this is why it makes sense to sell at market. And I collected
my money, 19 sous and 39. Then my oxen were sold. My
God! I don't know how much all this makes; if I were to put it
all into an account ("Se meïsse tout en .I. conte"), I wouldn't
know how to total it. . . . And nevertheless Sirous, who sold
and counted, told me that I got 50 sous for my oxen. But I
don't know if he lied, nor if he stole from me. For between my
2 setiers of wheat and my mare and my pig and the wool from
my sheep I made as much. 2 times 50 makes 100, said a guy
who did my accounts; he said that this came to 5 pounds. I
hope my purse which is as full as can be does not fall into
my lap."[37]

As the above long quotation makes clear, there can be no
difference between the tale (the *conte*) that one reads and Boi-
vin's invention. The wily merchant literally generates himself,

and the genealogy that he fabricates—and kills off at the same time—is predicated upon absence: "If only I had my sweet niece with me now . . . ," he laments, "she would be mistress of my wealth. . . . Oh sweet niece Mabile, you are of such good lineage. What could have possessed you to leave? For my three children are dead as is my wife Siersaut!" [38] Even the name Boivin adopts for the occasion—Fouchier de Brouce—suggests his fictitious status, his status as fiction, betraying as it does the character of the swindler (compare with "fauchier"), of the fornicator (compare with "foutier"), and of the trickster (compare with "fou-chier").

Self-creating economic and literary value coincide in Boivin's imaginary purse, as the identity of accounts and of the "conte" becomes the chief source of dramatic interest within the fabliau. [39] Both are, moreover, also assimilated to prostitution; and if Boivin embodies the image of the poet as inventor, Mabile, the prostitute, takes on the role of the reader, or misreader. Mistaking linguistic and monetary value, she cannot distinguish between that which is told ("raconté") and the false economic reckoning ("conte"), just as later Ysane will not be able to distinguish Boivin's purse ("borse") from his testicles ("borse") in what amounts to a fake dismemberment of the body through the dismemberment of language.

Like the confusion between accounts, the separation from purses or false castration casts the fabliaux in the mold of narrative competition between various protagonists, a competition that, once again, mirrors the rivalry between jongleurs. In both cases the one who invents the best tale triumphs over the others, as competing lies concerning sums of money, family, name, virginity, the fake gestures of generosity and of indignation, the costumes, props, and make-up come to constitute whatever can be affirmed with certainty about the fabliaux—that is, their function as performances. For the only moment of truth in "De Boivin de Provins," as in other similar tales, is already secondary and to be found in the retelling of the sum total—the account—of lies to the chief of police: "Boivin went right to the provost and told him the truth word for word from beginning to end" (*Recueil*, V, 64). [40] If Boivin is the poet ("qui cest fablel / fist à Provins"), and if Mabile is the inscribed reader, the provost can be identified with the patron, the one who pays for the telling: "Sovent li fist conter sa vie / A ses parens, à ses amis."

"De Boivin" and "Du Chevalier qui fist sa fame confesser" thematize the rivalry between jongleurs in terms of a rivalry between protagonists, each of whom tries to create the most credible fiction. Such an inscription of the genesis of the tale is only possible, however, because the poet himself is a trickster who, in exposing the creation of stories within the story, merely exposes himself. We have seen that poetry is identified with trickery in "Du Vilain au buffet," but the example is hardly unique. In "Des .II. Changeors," a story which turns around the staging of sexual betrayal, the poet notes that "Onques, nus hom, à mon avis, / Ne fu mès aussi desjouglez" (*Recueil*, I, 253). The wife of "Du Vilain de Bailleul" proceeds to deceive her husband by a brand of trickery so allied with jonglerie that the association could hardly have passed unnoticed: "Cele se haste, ne puet ains, / De lui deçoivre par sa jangle" (*Recueil*, IV, 214). So too the husband of "Le Dit dou soucretain" speaks a "false Latin" that is the equivalent of jonglerie: "Mès il parla mout faus latin, / Et les servi mout bien de gangles" (*Recueil*, VI, 124).

Poetry is a trick—a "trueve"; and as the author of "Sainte Léocade" contends, the art of the trouvère is that of the trickster.[41] Rutebeuf maintains in "De Charlot le juif," itself a tale of the duper duped, that "he who wants to deceive a performer must outdo him in cleverness; for often it happens that the one who thinks he has outfoxed a minstrel in the end finds that his purse has been cleaned."[42]

The word "menestrel," like "jongleur," stands not only as the designation of the performer, but as equivalent to "the deceiver" or "liar." Richeut, the "master of lechery" who represents "the height of debauchery," is also the "menestrel"; and her alternate appellation—Richart—suggests that she is literally "Rich(en)art."[43] The association of poetry and prostitution is, moreover, doubly significant, since there is no difference finally between the art of the "menestrel," the glorification of trickery within the fabliaux, and the idea of "turning a trick."

The poet as trickster culminates in the figure of Trubert who participates in practically every mode of scandal that we have seen thus far. Trubert is the fornicator who commits adultery with the wife of a man whom he also sodomizes; he is the coprophilist who covers with excrement the Duke who pays him for his services.[44] Trubert is an embodiment of the artist—the one who, having lived the series of adventure that we read, becomes capable of telling his own story (*Trubert*, vv. 2130ff.). And the one whose creations *ex nihilo* are transformed into value: to wit, the goat which he paints and manages to sell at an exorbitant price (*Trubert*, vv. 27–253) as well as the multiple coats that he receives as a reward for his capacity for illusion (*Trubert*, vv. 491, 1750, 2473). Like the medieval Merlin, of which he is a satyric version, Trubert is a "samblance." He is multiform. The plethora of disguises that he adopts transform him successively into a carpenter, doctor, and knight. A quick-change artist of the first order, Trubert is the transvestite ("et Trubert ne s'atarje mie, / une coife a fame a lacie") who also becomes a transsexual: "Il (Golias) est bien du tout enginiez: / ne set mie la traïson / de sa fame qui n'a pas con!"[45] He is finally a polyvalent scandalous shifter who, by his own admission, revels in trickery,[46] yet who, as a semblance devoid of substance, remains hidden—unrecognizable, unlocatable, undefinable, and unnamable; "nus ne puis savoir / qui je sui ne comment j'ai non," he brags, echoing Merlin's "c'est gent qui me cuident connoistre ne sevent riens de mon estre."[47] The question of how to name Trubert is indeed the crux of his relation to the diverse representations he stages. For among the multiple epithets the trickster elicits —"niais," "fobert," "tricheor," "trufeor," "li soz," "li bacheliers," "li bers," "li desloiaus," "li gloz"—none better subsumes the others than that of "li menestrés." *Trubert* is finally a homonym of *trobar*, the originless deceiver who stages the tale which obscures its own lack of origin.

THE FABLIAUX, FETISHISM, AND THE JOKE

Les éléments "qui les constituent réellement" reposent soit, dans la plupart des fabliaux et des fables, sur des donnés morales si générales qu'elles peuvent également être admises de tout homme, en un temps quelconque; soit, dans la plupart des contes de fées, sur un merveilleux si peu caractérisé qu'il ne choque aucune croyance, et peut être indifféremment accepté, à titre de simple fantaisie amusante, par un bouddhiste, un chrétien, un musulman, un fétichiste.

JOSEPH BÉDIER

We have an undefinable feeling, rather, which I can best compare with an "absence," a sudden release of intellectual tension, and then all at once the joke is there—as a rule ready-clothed in words.

SIGMUND FREUD

We have seen how closely the representation of the body in the fabliaux is linked to the theme of fragmentation—to detached members, both male and female; to actual and metaphoric castrations; but most of all, to metaphor as castration. In this the isolated body part as well as the circulating corpse implicate the nature of storytelling, as the fragmented body becomes a floating signifier which draws all who come into contact with it into the scandal of interpretation. Given the necessity of an always inadequate reading of the isolated body part, the implied reader is by definition guilty of a deforming illegitimacy. The ubiquitous theme of bodily dismemberment thus stands as the most manifest sign of a constant questioning of the sufficiency of poetic representation, which is also evident formally in the multiple modes of linguistic disruption to be found throughout the medieval comic tale—in word play; phonological, onomastic, and semantic misunderstanding; use of proverbs and extended metaphors; bilingualism.

If dismemberment of the body is, moreover, coterminous with the dismemberment of meaning, the dismemberment of meaning is the source of sexual desire. This is the point of the series of tales involving the deflected naming of sexual organs, tales which also reveal the extent to which sexual pleasure within the fabliaux is rooted neither in a naturalism of the body nor in that of language, but in a denaturing literary act. All of which leads us to the following tautology: a narrative fixation upon the partial at once engenders desire (as theme) and the desire for narrative. The desire of the poem for the poem is expressed in terms of the inscribed narrator who stages—from within—the tale which seems to spring from nowhere, or whose only identifiable source is internal. Ultimately, the difference between the tale within the tale and the narrative that we read is minimal; or for that matter, the difference between the rivalry of the inventors of internal fictions and rival jongleurs.

Such an assertion is more than a question of external literary history, the arguments of which the reader may have noticed I have avoided. The fact that of the approximately 170 fabliaux most are anonymous, that so many of the remaining 55 tales bear 30 otherwise unidentifiable names, and that most of these are stereotypical first names is incidental next to the explicitness with which the fabliaux represent their own genesis, the insistence with which they seem to deflect the question of an external origin toward that of how to tell the best tale.[1]

The fabliaux better than any other medieval form stage the problem of absence vis-à-vis their own genesis. The absence which they stage is, however, by no means arbitrary. On the contrary, the series of tales which explicitly make absences speak also make explicit the relation between the possibility of such speech and the castrated sexual member. We have already hinted at such a link in the suggestion that the knight's desire to hear his wife's confession in the tale by that same name is in reality a desire to hear her organ—or *con*—tell ("raconter") the truth of her (invented?) aventures. The vaginal attribution of poetic speech becomes even more apparent in "De Celle qui se fist foutre sur la fosse de son mari." Modeled upon the classical Matron of Ephesus (Petronius), this tale is predicated upon the absence of the dead husband whose tomb—"la *fosse du mari*"—is the womb that once belonged to him and is not filled. Such an absence is supplemented by a story invented, in this case, by a squire who bets his knight that he can seduce her. And seduce her he does with the following fabrication:

> "— Suer, je sui plus dolenz la disme.
> — Coment plus? — Jel te dirai, suer.
> Je avoie mis tout mon cuer
> En une dame que j'avoie,
> Et assez plus de moi l'amoie,
> Qui ert bele, cortoise et sage;
> Ocise l'ai par mon outrage.
> — Ocise l'as? Coment, pechierre?
> En foutant, voir, ma dame chiere,
> Ne je ne voudroie plus vivre.
> — Gentilz hon, vien ça, si delivre
> Cest siecle de moi, si me tue;
> Or t'en esforce et esvertue,
> Et si me fai, se tu pues, pis
> Que tu ta fame ne feïs;
> Tu dis qu'ele fu morte à foutre?"
>
> (*Recueil*, III, 121)

"— Sweet lady, I am ten times more disconsolate than you. — How's that? — I'll tell you. I had placed all my love in a lady I know. She was beautiful, courteous, and wise; and I loved her more than myself. But I killed her, by my excess. — You killed her? How's that, sinner? — By fucking, truly, my dear lady. Now I can no longer stand to live. — Noble man, come closer and deliver me from the world, kill me; make a little effort, and do to me worse than you did to your lady. You say she died fucking?"

The above exchange is symptomatic of the fact that it is not the desiring body that generates the tale which merely reflects it, but the tale which produces desire and which can even be held responsible for the desire for narrative. There is, again, nothing outside of the fabliau—no naked body of Nature beneath the cloak of representation—to sustain the search for origins, historical realism, or destination.

But let's continue with another example, "De Berengier au lonc cul." This tale of the boastful knight who rides out every morning, hangs up his shield, batters it, and returns with the account of his adventures—"as if he had done great feats" (*Recueil*, IV, 58)—also originates in an absence filled by pure invention. An absence, moreover, that is tantamount to castration; for when his wife discovers he is lying she herself dresses as a knight, rides into the forest, and confronts him with the possibility of a real battle. When he balks, she makes him kiss her backside:

> Si s'estupa devant sa face,
> Et cil vit une grant crevace
> Du cul et du con, ce li samble,
> Qui trestout se tenoit ensamble;
> Onques mais, se Dieus li aït,
> Ce dist, ausi lonc cul ne vit,
> Lors l'a besié et acliné.
>
> (*Recueil*, IV, 64)

She bent over before his face, and this one saw a large crevice from the anus to the vagina which, it seemed, all formed one ensemble. Never before, so help him God, he said, had he ever seen such a long crack; then he bent over and kissed it.

"Du Berengier au lonc cul" is a tale whose comic effect is constituted by an absence: that is, the husband's failure to realize that this is a woman—much less his own wife!—implies that he too has no testicles. Even this semblance of castration, however, is divested of origins; for as the wife explains, her name is without genealogy: "I assure you, you cannot find it anywhere around these parts; even my parents don't have it, for I am named Berengier of the Long Ass, and I shame all cowards."[2]

This is a fabliau whose moral intent by all reckoning is the denunciation of liars; the author concludes: "for this reason I advise all who brag and do not carry through with their

boasts to leave their bragging behind."[3] And yet, the very ve-
hicle of didactic intention is itself a lie, the savvy wife draped
in the ill-fitting cloak—the armor—of a knight. Nor is the
jongleur, by his own admission, any less of an inventor, a fab-
ricator of lies, than the mendacious husband: "Since I like to
tell fables and have put my mind to it, I cannot resist telling
you that it once happened in Lombardy. . . ."[4] "De Berengier
au lonc cul" is from the beginning a cover-up, the masking of
an absence whose origin or original point of reference is itself
invented.

The fabliaux make such absences speak, which is what the
series of tales concerning speaking vaginas is all about. We
have already encountered a hint of the motif of the garrulous
member in "Le Jugement des cons," a work whose comic
effect turns around the transfer of the reference of the title
from the woman's sexual organ to the woman herself. "Du
Con qui fu fait à la besche" assimilates the possibility of such
a transfer to the simultaneous creation of the vagina and of
crafty speech:

> La besche prent et si s'afiche,
> Tout enz jusqu'au manche la fiche.
> Ainsi fist le con à la besche:
> Vers la fame un petit s'abesse,
> Un pet li a fet sur la langue,
> Par ce a fame tant de jangle;
> Por ce borde-ele et jengle tant.[5]

He [the Devil] took the shovel and shoved it in up to the
hilt. Thus the cunt was made with a spade. Then he got
down to the woman's level and farted on her tongue, and it
is for this reason that she talks, jokes, and lies so much.

Then too, the incidental exchange between the Devil's anus
and the woman's mouth contained in "Du Con qui fu fait à la
besche" is given full-blown treatment in "Le Débat du con et
du cul": "The anus asked the cunt for 3 sous rent, but the cunt
maintained it did not owe so much. . . . 'What's this,' said the
anus, 'do you want to drive me nuts?'":[6]

"— Nenil, biaus amis," dist le Con
Je ne demant fors que mon droit.
Contons, moi et toi orendroit,
Et si sauras que je te doi.
— Par foi," dist li Cus, "Je l'otroie;
Je conterai moult volentiers.
Ne me dois-tu .XII. deniers
Quant tu eschaufes et tu sues;
Por ce que dout que tu ne pues,
Je te corne, je te deduis,
Je te souffle au mieux que je puis;
Je t'abandone tout mon vent?
Ce sont .II. sous; or me les rent."
Et dis li Cons: "Tu contes bien. . . ."

(*Recueil*, II, 133–34)

"— Not at all, sweet friend," said the cunt. "I'm only asking for my due. Let us count now, you and I, and you will know what I owe you. — By faith," said the anus, "I grant it; I'll count willingly. Don't you owe me 12 deniers for when you heat up and sweat. In order that you not stink I blow you off and refresh you; I breathe on you as best I can. Don't I give you all my wind? That alone is worth 2 sous, so give them to me." Then the cunt said, "You count well. . . ."

In the counting of the vagina and the anus we recognize the accounting of the poet who plays upon the homophony of *con* and *con*te ("contons," "conterai," "contes"). The debate between adjacent body parts is, at bottom, that of the jongleur who, in addressing his audience, manages to make *cons* and *culs* speak:

"A toz cels dont tu es amez
Doinst Dame Diex male aventure,
Quar il font *con*tre nature;
Qui me lessent et à toi vont,
Je pri Dieu que il les *con*font.
Je faz agenoillier les *con*tes,
Les chastelains et les vis*con*tes; . . .

> Je les faz metre à estupons
> Et redrecier à re*cul*ons. . . ."
>
> (*Recueil*, II, 135)

May God condemn all who love you, for they do it
against nature. Those who leave me and go to you I pray
to God that he will confound them. I cause to kneel
counts, lords, and viscounts; . . . I get them to crouch
and to straighten out backing up. . . .

The poet is the one who, by animating the disputation that by
his own admission comes from nowhere ("Seignor, ceste de-
sputison, / Qu'avez oï du Cul et du Con, / Si m'avint en
l'autrier en sonjant" [*Recueil*, II, 136]) fills with the word for
absence itself the absence par excellence: "Mès onques plus je
n'en oï / Fors ce que j'ai *conté* ci" (II, 136).

This thesis is most evident in the title of a tale that in many
respects sums up the problem at hand. "Du Chevalier qui fist
les cons parler" is the story of a vassal literally uncovered by
years of economic hardship, divested of even a "mantel mau-
taillié": "For this knight had spent all he had; . . . he pos-
sessed neither a coat of ermine, nor an outer coat, nor a fur
hat, nor a penny's worth of other goods, since he had hocked
it all."[7] The destitute knight's situation is reversed by his
squire's theft of maidens' clothing while they are bathing; for
in the cover-up of this scandal, the restoration of stolen gar-
ments and the recloaking of naked bodies, he receives super-
natural gifts. The first maiden bestows upon him the power
always to be entertaining for money:

> "Jamais en cel lieu ne venroiz
> Que toz li monz ne vos enjoie,
> Et chascun fera de vos joie;
> Et si vos abandoneront
> La gent trestot quanqu'il aront:
> Ne porroiz mais avoir poverte."
>
> (*Recueil*, VI, 75)

"Never will you enter a place without amusing those
who are there; and each will make you happy, for they
will give you all they have."

The second maiden grants him the power to make absences speak:

> "Ja n'ira mès ne loig ne près,
> Por qu'il truisse feme ne beste,
> Et qu'el ait deus elz en la teste,
> S'il daigne le con apeler,
> Qu'il ne l'escoviegne parler."
>
> (*Recueil*, VI, 75)

"Never will you wander so far or wide that you will find a woman or beast who has two eyes in her head and whose cunt, if you dare to address it, will not respond."

The third promises that if by chance the vagina is prevented from speaking, "the anus will respond in its place" ("Que se li cons, par aventure, / Avoit aucun enconbrement . . . / Li cus si respondroit par lui" [VI, 76]).[8]

The knight's magic gifts tempt us to see in him the author of "Le Dialogue du con et du cul" since he dialogues so freely with the genitals of a rich priest's mare and then with the anus of a countess who has stuffed her vagina with cotton in order to prevent just such a conversation.

But what are the bestowed powers if not those of the poet or jongleur? The author of the fabliau achieves exactly what is attributed to the knight; he makes *cons* speak:

> Ne sai que feïsse lonc *con*te:
> En cel chastel avoit un *con*te
> Et la *con*tesse avuec, sa feme, . . .
> De maintenant el chastel entre
> Cil qui faisoit les *con*s paller.
> Tuit le corrurent saluer,
> Qui mout le vuelent *con*joïr,
> Dont il se puet mout esjoïr.
> En mi la vile uns gieus avoit
> Où li pueples trestot estoit:
> Si ert li *quen*s et la *con*tesse, . . .
> Atant li chevaliers i vint, . . .
> Au *con*te, meïsme fu tart
> Qu'acolé l'ait et enbracié,

Enz en la bouche l'a baisié.
Ausi l'enbrace la *con*tesse;
Plus volantiers que n'oïst messe
Le baisast vint fois près à près,
Se li *con*tes ne fust si près.
Et cil descent *con*tre la gent; . . .
A grant joie l'en ont mené
Tot droit à la sale le *con*te.
Puis ne firent pas lonc a*con*te. . . .

(*Recueil*, VI, 79–80)[9]

The knight makes vaginas talk in exchange for money, as the countess, who has wagered that hers is mute, pays off; this is where the tale ends: "A tant est li *con*te finez" (VI, 89). Similarly, the poet makes *con*s speak and—through the equivalent of *con*crete poetry!—is richly rewarded; this, in fact, is where the tale begins: "Flabel sont or mout entorsé; / Maint denier en ont enborsé / Cil qui les *con*tent et portent" (VI, 68). ("Fabliaux are very twisted these days, and many a penny has been earned by those who tell and carry them around.")

"Du Chevalier qui fist les cons parler" drives home the points that I have been making all along: the fabliaux inscribe their own origin in such a way as to render absurd the questions of source, authorial identity, and destination; this origin is marked by an absence that is particularly poignant in tales involving vaginal speech; this absence is synonymous with a castration—both a bodily dismemberment and the dismemberment of language; and finally, this castration is assimilable to the contingent, partial, fragmentary nature of narrative itself. Or, to follow such a train of thought to its logical conclusion, the fabliaux, perhaps better than any other Old French genre, demonstrate the extent to which desire is at once produced by the tale, in the tale, and for the tale. This amounts to saying that there can be no difference between the desire so often expressed in sexual terms on the level of theme and the desire for the story itself. The homophony in Old French between the word for vagina and for narrative (or, in English, the tail and the tale) signifies the closeness of physical and linguistic longings. "Seignor, qui les bons cons savez, / Qui savez que li cons est tels / Que il demande sa droiture" (*Recueil*, II, 137)—thus begins "Le Dit des cons" in which Gautier le Loup or le Leu (whose name denotes both the ruse of wolf and the place of speech) conflates the law of literature and of sex that becomes quite simply synonymous with the law: "Contre le con ne vaut engin" (*Recueil*, VI, 139).

The text's resistance to traditional literary historical categories takes us in another direction altogether, one that has hovered in the margins of our discussion from the beginning. Its recalcitrance enables us to move beyond the struggle with "philological windmills," beyond the light which any given tale might shed upon the status of poetry at the end of the Middle Ages. For the issues which have shaped our reading throughout—a certain playing with the power of representation both to reveal and to conceal, bodily dismemberment, loss of linguistic property, the inscription of sexual desire within such problems of loss, and the relation of the erotic and the poetic—suggest a link between the fabliaux and that peculiarly modern solicitation of speech and cash: psychoanalysis. Indeed, the reader the least bit familiar with psychoanalytic thought must long before now have sensed how explicitly—and naturally—the fabliaux seem "to speak" and "to *make* speak" questions central to Freudian and post-Freudian analysis.

The setting of the medieval text against the contemporary discourse which it seems not so much to reflect as to animate is, moreover, a critical move whose own meaning lies less in the domain of illustration of something like a universal or "human nature" than in the displacements which a textual corpus like the fabliaux is itself capable of working upon the canons of modernism. Here again, the thematics which I have solicited from even such a partial grouping of tales suggests a powerful connection between the kind of narrative elaboration characteristic of the fabliaux, the "castration complex," fetishism, and the comic.

There is, first of all, a long historical association beginning with Aristotle between the comic and the phallic, comedy or "low songs" and the *ithyphalloi* or *phallophoroi*. There is, further, and this again from the very beginning, a tendency to associate comedy and bodily deformity. Plato emphasizes the "kinship of the ridiculous with what is morally or physically faulty"; Aristotle claims it represents "a kind of failing or deformity which is not painful or injurious to others." Later rhetoricians such as Demetrius and the author of the *Coislinian Treatise* insist that "the jester ridicules faults of mind and body." Comedy is rooted in the defective, in Aristotle's "representation of men as worse than they are"—in the partial and particular as opposed to the universal of tragedy. More important, that which provokes laughter always involves a cutting short, a foreshortening. This is a point stressed persistently by those who have undertaken the task of writing seriously about humor. The Shakespearian adage according to which "Brevity is the soul of wit" is echoed over and over again. Kant claims in the *Critique of Aesthetic Judgement* that "laughter is an 'affection' arising from a strained expectation suddenly reduced to nothing." George Meredith (*The Egoist*) maintains that comedy is the function that allows compression of whole sections of the Book of Ego into a sentence, volumes into a chapter; it is "a means of reading quickly." Freud insists at considerable length that jokes are economical; they imply a certain short-circuiting of psychic energy.[10]

Nor can such foreshortening be detached from the slippages, displacements, condensations, and substitutions that are the proper of jokes. The joke cuts, and it cuts short, which is why Freud loves jokes about tailors and why the one about the displaced blacksmith, repeated both in *Jokes and Their Relation to the Unconscious* and *The Ego and the Id*, takes on such exemplary status. This is the tale of a Hungarian town in which the blacksmith had been guilty of a capital offense. "The Burgomaster, however, decided that as a penalty a tailor should be hanged, because there were two tailors in the village but no second blacksmith, and the crime must be expiated."[11] The replacement of the blacksmith by the tailor captures the essence of the "joke-work" (itself a joke?), which implies a shortcut, a diversion, the displacement of an initial topic by a second one, as well as a substitution. But what, it may be asked, is displaced? What slips? What is the nature of the substitute?

A partial answer to these questions lies in Freud's assertion that "the brevity of jokes is often the outcome of a particular process which has left behind in the wording of the joke a second trace—the formation of a substitute. By making use of the procedure of reduction . . . we also find, however, that the joke depends entirely on its verbal expression as established by the process of condensation" (*JU*, p. 28). Not only does a cutter of cloth replace a forger, but such a replacement implies a linguistic displacement as well: "a joke contains nothing more than a word capable of multiple meaning, which allows the hearer to find the transition from one thought to another" (*JU*, p. 54).

In its cutting the joke involves a loss operative both at the level of the person about whom it is told and the process of telling. The question of what is lost is thus more complicated than at first glance. The answer cannot be the blacksmith, for he survives. Nor can it be the tailor, since this is a joke which turns around the fact that tailors are expendable; and as long as one survives, they are also interchangeable. What is lost in the splitting of individual fate along the lines of social usefulness rather than according to actual guilt is something like an assumed notion of proper justice. Which raises the question of can there be a proper substitution of the type contained in the tailor joke? Is the joke—any joke—thinkable without this or an equivalent substitution? If the joke "depends entirely upon verbal expression," is language not ultimately its proper object, or a certain assumption of verbal propriety which is displaced, lost, substituted for?

The range of comic techniques that Freud outlines, and his list (*JU*, pp. 41–42) is as good as any, is strikingly similar to that we have designated for the fabliaux. Like the humor of the medieval tale, the effectiveness of the joke seems always to imply an ill-tailoring of "verbal expression," a violence done to words; and this right down to the level of the letter. The "joke-work" may, for instance, involve condensation with formation of a composite word, as in the famous example of *familiär* and *Millionär* combined to produce *familionär*, or *alcohol* and *holidays* to yield *alcoholidays*. The joke cuts words in unexpected places, as in the multiple use of the same word as a whole and in parts, e.g., the characterization of a red-haired, silly relative to Jean-Jacques Rousseau as *roux et sot*, or the response to the medical questionnaire concerning masturbation—"O, na, nie!" ("Oh, no, never!") An analogous process is to found in: the use of the same words full and empty ("*Eifersucht* [jealousy] is a *Leidenschaft* [passion] which *mit Eifer sucht* [with eagerness seeks] what *Leiden schaft* [causes pain]); the use of the same words in a different order ("Mr. and Mrs. X live in a fairly grand style. Some people say that the husband has earned a lot and so has been able to lay by a bit; others that the wife has lain back a bit and so has been able to earn a lot"); or the use of the same word with slight modification ("Herr N. heard a gentleman who was born a Jew make a spiteful remark about a Jewish character. 'Herr Hofrat,' he said, 'your ant*e*semitism was well-known to me; your ant*i*semitism is new'").

Alongside the usual cuts, condensations, and substitutions that jokes work at the level of the letter are the displacements of sense or breaks in reference which are synonymous with humor as word play. These include: double meaning as a word and as a thing ("'Why,' it was asked, in times that are now past, 'have the French rejected Lohengrin?' 'On Elsa's [Alsace] account'"); double meaning arising from literal and metaphorical understanding (e.g., the priest's invocation to charity in "De Brunain la vache au prestre"); *double entendre* ("Have you taken a bath? No, is one missing?"); and double meaning proper (e.g., the famous remark concerning Napoleon III's disappropriation, upon assuming power, of the property of the House of Orléans: "C'est le premier vol de l'aigle").[12]

In the substitution of one proper for another, of the improper for the proper, in the cutting of words in unexpected places, and in their unusual combination, the joke displaces an assumed linguistic propriety characteristic of its initial premise; and in this replacement of the expectation of sense by a "second trace" it is logic that is implicated. Indeed, there is a long tradition which perceives logic and laughter as mutually exclusive. This incompatibility, again present from the beginning in the Greek association of the *phallophoroi* and the *sophistai*, is perhaps best expressed by Schopenhauer who maintains in *The World as Will and Idea* that laughter originates in the incongruity between conception and perception, between abstraction (or belief) and experience, which can itself be reduced to the following logical (and unfunny) terms: everything funny can be traced to a certain syllogism in the first figure, "or an undisputed *major* (thesis) and an unexpected minor, which to a certain extent is only sophistically valid, in consequence of which connection the conclusion partakes of the quality of the ludicrous."[13] Comedy is, then, a kind of exemplification of the perception that nothing actual is wholly logical, nothing finite infinite, nothing limited ideal.

This is another way of saying that though the joke may replace a blacksmith by a tailor, it is the expectation of sense that is displaced by the joke. To wit, one of Freud's favorites: "A. borrowed a kettle from B. and, after he had returned it was sued by B. because the kettle now had a big hole in it which made it unusable. His defense was: 'First, I never borrowed a kettle from B. at all; secondly, the kettle had a hole in it already when I got it from him; and thirdly, I gave him the kettle undamaged'."

Like the kettle, the joke is itself filled with holes despite the semblance of coherence of the whole. Rather, it maintains a double logic according to which it is no longer possible to distinguish the presupposition of the beginning from the only "sophistically valid" defenses which contradict it as well as each other. The joke cuts, and it cuts both ways, which is why it so often gives the impression of a superior logic capable of recuperating even its own contradiction:[14] "An impoverished individual borrowed 25 florins from a prosperous acquaintance, with many asservations of his necessitous circumstances. The very same day his benefactor met him again in a restaurant with a plate of salmon mayonnaise in front of him. The benefactor reproached him: 'What? You borrow money from me and then order yourself salmon mayonnaise? Is *that* what you've used my money for?' 'I don't understand you,' replied the object of the attack; 'if I haven't any money I *can't* eat salmon mayonnaise, and if I have some money I *mustn't* eat salmon mayonnaise. Well, then when *am* I to eat salmon mayonnaise?'."

The double logic of the joke betrays a persistent tension between the independent validity of each defense (whether against the charge of breaking pots or of profligacy) despite their mutual incompatibility; and it suggests a willful forgetting or blindness that in the course of the telling becomes apparent. The comic, in fact, produces in the reader (or listener) the feeling of "having failed to see," of "having always known," or at least of "having been capable of knowing."

This is the lesson of several fabliaux which focus on the problem of vision. "Les .III. Avugles," as we have seen, turns around the difference between perceptual and conceptual knowledge of the absence of the coin, as the three blind men with mutually exclusive explanations debate under only "sophistically valid" premises the whereabouts of the money.[15] The tale is in fact about how they learn that which they could and should have surmised all along. All of which transforms blindness into a metaphor for the way humor works. For both the tavern keeper and the parish priest, despite their faculty of sight, are, like blind men, unable to see the ruse of the knight. The comic effect of the second half of the fabliau consists precisely in their gradual perception of that which was available conceptually from the beginning: the fact that words are the only coin exchanged. In this manner too the audience comes to occupy the position of all who are duped, since for the duration of the performance they remain incapable of seeing that the ruse of the knight is that of the poet—the illusion of complicity, or the dupery of the displacement of dupery upon the Other.

Another parable of blindness is to be found in "Du Prestre qui abevete" ("The Spying Priest"). This is the tale of a priest who, looking through the keyhole of a peasant's front door, begins an argument about the relation between what he sees and what the couple is doing:

> "— Mengiés, faites? vous i mentés,
> Il m'est avis que vous foutés.
> — Taisiés, sire, nous faisons voir:
> Nous mengons, ce poés voir."
> Dist li prestres: "Je n'en dout rien,

> Vous foutés, car je le voi bien,
> Bien me volés avuler."
>
> (Recueil, III, 55)

"— Eating, you say? You are lying. I think I saw you fucking. — Hush, sir, we were acting honestly: we were eating, this much you could see." The priest said: "I don't doubt a bit that you were fucking, since I saw it. You are trying to blind me."

To test the truth of conflicting contentions the priest convinces the peasant to step outside and see for himself. He in turn enters the house, fornicates with the peasant's wife, and defends himself with the claim, like that of his adversary in the beginning, to have been eating.

"Du Prestre qui abevete" contains a quarrel over who can see and who cannot. It is a staging of blindness where the humor depends on a persistent gap between conception and perception that becomes increasingly humorous through reversal—i.e., the priest's false accusation of fornication versus the peasant's true perception of eating transformed into the priest's false perception of eating versus the peasant's true accusation of fornication. The essence of the fable is the logical impossibility of reducing to univocity conflicting accounts of what is seen, or the realization that to the extent to which the peasant manages to make his vision stick he is a cuckold:

> "— Par le cuer Dieu, ce samble fable",
> Dist li vilains, "ja nel creïse,
> S'anchois dire nel vous oïsce,
> Que vous ne foutissiés ma famme.
> — Non fach, sire, taisiés; par m'ame,
> Autrestel sambloit ore à moi."
>
> (Recueil, III, 56)

"— By the heart of God, this appears to be a fable," said the peasant, "I never would have believed, if I had not heard you say it, that you were not fucking my wife. — Hush, I'm not, sir; by my soul it seemed like that to me when I was outside."

Blindness works like a puzzle, and the fabliau stands as the narrative account of an unraveling of that which was accessible only enigmatically from the start. In this the sensation of fore-shortening or of a short circuit of psychic energy is the feeling of having always already known. Herein lies the point of the joke of jokes—shortcut of shortcuts—in which prisoners, after long years of confinement, merely mention the numbers of various humorous tales in order to break out laughing. Herein too the meaning of the joke that Theodore Reik claims to have heard from Freud: [16] "A certain patient in a mental institution had argued long and hard that he must be served only kosher food. Finally, unable to avoid the extra work and expense, the director of the institution acquiesced. A few days later, on the Sabbath, the director was strolling around the grounds, when he came upon the same patient sitting in a chair and smoking a cigar. 'Wait a minute, Schwartz,' he said. "I thought you were so religious that we had to bring in special food for you. And now, here you are smoking on the Sabbath!' 'But Doctor,' Schwartz replied. 'Did you forget? I'm *meshugah*!'" The secret of the joke-work is that it makes us work to see that which is visible from the beginning. Like the doctor, the hearer forgets that which he clearly knew all along and which is the condition of the possibility of listening to any comic story—that the joke, like the patient, is crazy.

In the course of the history of writing on the comic, thinkers have maintained alternately that humor implies both blindness and something akin to total vision. Vico, for instance, claims that to see the truth is to see nothing humorous; "but second-rate minds, which see things only partially, are inclined to recognize the ludicrous." For Nietzsche, on the other hand, Zarathustra laughs as deeply as he does because he is able on high to see all. What our analysis suggests, in contrast, is that the joke implies neither in any absolute sense. Rather, it sustains an always uneasy balance between the expectation of continuity, of sense, and the discovery of the limits of this initial premise; both of which are recuperated finally by the reinscription of a "logic of the joke" based upon the intrinsically irreconcilable copresence of conception and perception. [17]

Now what is intriguing about this particular logical configuration is that it seems surprisingly connected to another and deadly serious area of psychoanalytic thought—that is, the oedipal complex. More precisely, it points to a link between the comic, primary narcissism, and fetishism that makes the transition between bodily dismemberment and humor and that takes us into the domain of the joke's social effect.

To begin, the ego's expectation of a meaningful whole that we have identified with the initial premise of the joke represents an essentially narcissistic investment in the continuity of the Self and the Other based upon the child's belief that "all persons he knows are possessed of genitals like his own."[18] A belief in the ubiquity of the phallus by analogy accounts for the presupposition of logic. And where the joke is concerned it is just such an expectation of linguistic and logical continuity—of sense—that is displaced—cut short, foreclosed—by the substitution of a "second trace." Thus the joke serves less to enable a regressive tapping of infantile pleasure through the aggression of others, as Freud would have it, or to enable the recovery of lost bodily grace, as Henri Bergson maintains, than to disrupt the narcissistic belief in the lack of difference between the Self and the Other. This means that when we say that the joke cuts, we mean it castrates (this despite Freud's effort to combine the *disjecta membra* of previous theories of humor into "an organic whole" [*JU*, p. 14]); and when we say the joke cuts both ways, we posit the comic as a cultural model akin to fetishism.[19]

Fetishism and the comic encroach upon one another at two points in Freud's writings. *Three Essays on Sexuality* and *Jokes and Their Relation to the Unconscious* were written simultaneously; the essay entitled "Fetishism" and the small article entitled "Humour" were produced in successive weeks of August, 1927. Such a coincidence of preoccupations is, however, anecdotal next to the fact that the key moment in the discovery of fetishism is the moment at which Freud understood that the fetish is linked to the forgetting of a maternal tongue: "The most remarkable case was that of a man who had created as a condition of the fetish a certain 'shine on the nose.' The surprising explanation was the fact that, raised in an English nursery, this patient later came to Germany where he forgot almost completely his maternal tongue (*Muttersprache*). The fetish whose origin was situated in early childhood was not to be understood in German but in English. The 'shine on the nose' (*Glanz auf der Nase*) was in reality a 'glance at the nose.'"[20] Fetishism, a forgetting of what is known from the beginning, implies the displacement of a proper designation by a "second trace," a castration of language and substitution for the proper par excellence: "The fetish is a substitute for the penis . . . a substitute for the phallus of the woman (the mother) in which the child once believed and which, as we know well why, he does not want to give up" ("Fetishism," p. 199).

Fetishism is synonymous with hiding, obfuscation, a scotomization or blindness associated, at least in Freudian terms, with a specific blind spot—the disavowal of knowledge of the mother's castration alongside of the forgetting of a mother tongue. The fetish is a *stigma indelebile* of repression, a cover whose own source lies not only in the magic of a supernatural coat (a "mantel mautaillié"), but in the very notion of fiction.

The facetious and the factitious are allied.[21] Over and above the original anthropological—totemic—function of the fetish, the semantic field of the word (from the Portuguese *feitiso* and the equivalent of the Latin *factitius*) transmits the notion of a "construction," "artifice," "fabrication," as well as the idea of an "imitation by signs."[22] As a "second trace" and substitute for the phallus of the mother, the fetish becomes "the first model of all repudiations of reality."[23] It is, further, the attempt to maintain the conceptual fiction of the feminine phallus despite the perceptual knowledge of its absence that accounts for the defining drama of socialization, the "resolution" of the oedipal struggle, or the renunciation of the object of narcissistic desire (as well as the presupposition that the Other is the Same) and the installation of a third term—the superego—to "cover" the other two. Through a substitution of the partial object for the feminine phallus and of a symbolic order for an imaginary one, fetishism represents the means by which the entire body is castrated or genitally focused and by which the law is incorporated. Like the 100 ladies of "Du Mantel mautaillié," the child is both covered and exposed by an internalized fiction—an ill-fitting coat—synonymous with a cleavage between an inner and outer, private and public, self which is the *sine qua non* of social life.[24] This splitting also removes fetishism from the narrow realm of perversion or of psychosis and makes of the process a general model of the defenses "coextensive with the psychoanalytic definition of the self."[25]

Here is where the socializing function of fetishism joins the socially recuperative thrust of the joke; for the comic tale works not, as Freud (and Bergson) would have it, only to subvert the social, but to reinforce it as well. This essentially conservative impetus is, of course, implicit to the numerous incipits and explicits that constitute the fabliaux at both ends as a didactic form. And it is specifically linked throughout the genre to the theme of dismemberment. Behind every beating is a lesson to be learned;[26] and behind every castration, a reimposition of the law. Thus the moral of "De Connebert" and that of "Du Prestre crucifié"—exemplary tales of castrated priests. And thus the pervasive sense that certain of the fabliaux read like Freudian parables: that is, they connect dismemberment, obfuscation, and the reimposition of the law; and they render explicit the extent to which the representation of this nexus at the level of theme embeds the act of storytelling within such a symbolic exercise of power.

A tale like "Du Sot Chevalier," for example, presents a scenario of maturation that seems in places like a literary version of the psychoanalytic account of infantile sexual discovery and socialization. For if the knight is naive or "sot," it is because he is so completely innocent of the difference between the male and female genitalia ("N'onques n'ot à fame géu, / Ne ne savoit que cons estoit" [*Recueil*, I, 221]) that, despite bodily contact, he remains incapable of sexual arousal:

> Mès cil n'avoit tant de savoir
> Qu'il séust au con adrecier,
> Ne le pucelage percier;
> Ne porquant l'avoit-il tenue
> Par maintes foiz trestoute nue.
>
> (*Recueil*, I, 221)

But he was so ignorant that he did not know how to approach [literally, "become erect to"] the cunt nor puncture a maidenhead; this despite the fact that he had held her completely nude many times.

How Freud would have loved "Du Sot Chevalier" which seems to speak the fetishistic fable! It is, as we have seen, a direct look at the genitals of the woman that engenders desire and that brings the childlike husband under the law of sexual difference. And in what remains one of the rare mentions of homosexuality in the fabliaux, the mother-in-law's lesson in "two holes" ("Gardez là ne voist vostre vis, / Quar il n'est pas à cel oés fais; / Qui vit i met, c'est granz meffais" [*Recueil*, I, 222]) is the event that signals a renunciation of narcissistic desire, or of the knight's lack of consciousness of the Other. This lifting of the oblique mother's skirt also transforms her into a trouvère, the specialist in "cons" and "contes" who, as an inscription of the poet, ends up recounting the tale of misadventure: "Ele tout l'afère lor conte; / Si leur a aconté le conte" (*Recueil*, I, 230). As suggested in closing, the fabliau does to the reader what the wife's mother does to her son-in-law: "Et li sot apris à foutre. / A cest mot est mon fablel outre" (I, 230).

"De Berengier au lonc cul," as we have also seen, is based upon the symbolic castration of a mendacious husband who, like the ingénu of "Du Sot Chevalier" and the everyboy of the Freudian oedipal fable, gazes directly upon the woman's *fundus* which he assumes to belong to a knight who has lost his testicles. Further, one consequence of the husband's fear of a similar fate is his submission to that which he fears: "Be quiet," says his wife lying in bed with her lover, "be sure you never mention this. For if you speak any further of it, I will that very morning without delay fetch Sir Berengier of the Long Ass who through his great power will take care of you." [27] It is, in other words, a staging of castration that brings the deceitful husband under the law and that makes his wife's invention of a powerful castrator assimilable to the invention of the comic tale.

An inversion of "De Berengier" which nonetheless makes an identical point is to be found in "Du Pescheor du pont seur Saine," a tale in which the conjugal power struggle of the beginning ("Il estoit sire et ele dame / De lui et de quanqu'il avoit" [*Recueil*, III, 68]) culminates in the wife's disparaging of her husband's member and in his dismemberment of a drowned priest. The staged presentation of the severed organ ("Le vit a geté en mi l'aire, / Et cele l'a bien regardé" [III, 72]) again serves to reestablish difference within the household. Through an initially metaphoric castration and the literal return of the phallus the entire household is recuperated under the paternal law: "Lors le commence à acoler, / A besier et à langueter, / Et tint la main au vit toz dis."[28]

The prime example of the fabliau as a parable of dismemberment and reintegration of the law is, of course, "De la Dame escoilliée." For here, as in "Du Pescheor du pont seur Saine" and "De Berengier," the tale originates in domestic crisis: the husband acknowledges not only that his wife "contradicts all that he says and undoes all that he does," but that she has "power over him": "De sor moi a la seignorie" (*Recueil*, VI, 98).[29] The wife's contestations of his authority range from the selection of food, to decisions concerning hospitality, and finally, to the choice of a husband for their daughter. The knight she picks, and who understands his father-in-law's dilemma, mutilates a disobedient hound (VI, 104), a willful horse (VI, 105), and the cook who mixes his sauces (VI, 107) in what amounts to a series of symbolic dismemberments. But the most significant of all is the mock castration of his mother-in-law staged with all the trappings of farce: the knight sends the rest of the family away, he orders a bull to be slaughtered and the testicles brought to him in a bowl which he hides under the table, he throws her down pretending to seek the source of her pride, and, finally:

> Son poig i met enz, et tot clos
> Un des coillons au tor mout gros
> Ça et là tire, et ele brait.
> Semblant fet que du cors li trait.
>
> (*Recueil*, VI, 112)

He thrust his fist in and grabbed one of the testicles by the thick part; he pulls here and there, and she screams. He pretended to pull it out of her body.

Though the above passage is idiosyncratic enough to be in-
teresting in and of itself, what remains significant is neither
the cleverness of the knight's ruse nor the phenomenon of fe-
male castration nor even the fact that its victim believes the
bull's testicles to be her own, but that castration presented as a
ruse engenders submission:

> Et cele cuide tot enfin
> Que ce soit voirs; et il li repasse.
> Et ele dit: "Chaitive! lasse!
> Com je fui de pute heure née,
> Desormès serai plus senée.
> Se de ci eschaper pooie,
> Mon seignor mès ne desdiroie."
>
> (*Recueil*, VI, 112)

And this one believes finally that all this is true; and he
repeats it again. And she says, "Woe is me! Alas! I was
born under an unlucky star. But from now on I will be
wiser. If I can escape from this, I will never contradict
my lord again."

The wife's belief in her own dismemberment is sufficient to
bring her under the paternal law, just as the mimetic repetition
of the scene of mutilation—its representation—produces a
similar effect in her daughter: "'I promise you,' she swears to
her husband, 'I will do whatever you want; if I don't, you can
cut my head off.' Then the count said, 'That's enough for now,
but if you are rebellious toward me, your balls will be re-
moved, as we did to your mother; for you should know that it
is only because of their nuts that women are disobedient and
silly.'"[30]

What, it may be asked, is the role of the text in such an im-
probable parable of dismemberment and submission? Hints
abound. For just as mother and daughter come, through the
representation of a semblance of castration, to fear the count
("Cremez vostre seignor le conte" [*Recueil*, VI, 103], "Et ne-
quedent le conte crient" [VI, 109]), the count becomes indis-
sociable from the account that we read and that, like fetishism
itself, engenders a double truth. That is, despite our con-
sciousness of the fable's status as fiction, we submit to it; be-

yond the willful illusion that is the premise of reading lies an essentially recuperative mediatory effect: "Teus est de cest flabel la some; / Dahet feme qui despit home!" (VI, 116).

Thus "De la Dame escoilliée" returns us to the area of fetishism, which turns precisely around the question of castrated women. For like the tale, the fetishist—and everyone is in this respect a fetishist—maintains a double truth: "His act reconciles two incompatible affirmations: the woman has kept her penis and the father has castrated her" ("Fetishism," p. 204). He is a "doubleur" who, like the peasant couple in "De Brunain la vasche au prestre," gets two for one; he both has his lie and believes it too. More important, the logic of fetishism— the balance of conception and perception, belief and knowledge, prejudice and vision—is none other than that of the joke. The reconciliation of "incompatible affirmations" reproduces the movement of Freud's kettle story. In the independent validity of each defense, despite their mutual incompatibility, we recognize the strategy of the fetishist who, in the succinct phrase of O. Mannoni, "knows all too well . . . but just the same. . . ."[31] But what has the implicit tragedy of the oedipal drama to do with the seeming frivolity of humor? Where in the topology of the mind can they possibly meet? What analogous function can they perform?

Here we must remember that the joke too "knows all too well . . . but just the same. . . ." And if the fetish is duplicitous, at once a monument to repression and, according to Freud, a "token of triumph over the threat of castration," ("Fetishism," p. 200), so too the joke serves a double purpose: it both cuts and forms a substitute experienced as what Hobbes terms the "sudden glory" of laughter. Humor is duplicitous not only in the sense of Jean Paul's "disguised priest who weds every couple," but in the sense of Freud's "double-dealing rascal" whose very purpose is to maintain the principle of duplicity. Hence the poignance of the one about the two Jews who meet in a railway station: "'Where are you going?' asks the first. 'To Pinsk,' replies the second. 'If you tell me you are going to Pinsk,' retorts the first, 'it means you are going to Minsk; and if you want me to believe you are going to Minsk, it means you are really going to Pinsk. So why lie?'" Indeed, the question one must ask of the joke is why lie? What is it lying about? What does the joke serve to hide?

The responses to these questions are as contradictory as the joke itself. Indeed the history of writing about the comic is the history of contradiction and points overall to a divergence between those who claim that humor hides our profoundly social nature, and thus plays the role of censor, and those who see in it one possibility for the subversion of the social. Across the ages there has been an extraordinary lack of consensus between those who have maintained alternately that laughter is overly logical or completely illogical, produced by partial or whole vision, dependent upon a displacement from something significant to the insignificant or from something insignificant to the significant, wholly linguistic or part of the object, a symptom of anxiety or a defense against anxiety, etc.[32] The joke is, again, none of the above and all of them—a hybrid. Like the structure of its own double logic, it serves at once as a form of revenge of the repressed, a lifting of our social self, and as "the most social of all the mental functions that aim at a yield of pleasure" (*JU*, p. 159). The joke-work is a regression that, unlike the dream-work, depends for its effect upon a socially defined intelligibility. It is, further, precisely the impossibility of defining the comic in terms other than those of a simultaneous copresence of opposites that allies it with the double truth of fetishism. Serving at the same time both to affirm and subvert, the comic is a transitional phenomenon much like Winnicott's transitional object—a potential space between the symbolic and the real, between the imaginary and the symbolic, between a certain bodily grace and rigidity, at once against the law and on the side of the law.[33]

The joke is a liminal phenomenon. Mauron situates it between the "anguish of tragedy and a return to everyday life"; Lacan, at the "precise point at which sense is produced from nonsense."[34] Weber places the joke at the center of the psychoanalytic canon because it is a "straddler" ("Aufsitzer") and because it is so resistant: "Jokes function in a manner very reminiscent of the discourse of the analyst, who refuses to engage in a meaningful dialogue with the analysand precisely in order to confront the latter with the desires that motivate questions in search of an answer."[35] Falling on the side neither of the regressive personal nor on that of the repressive social, the joke straddles a double truth which, as the fabliaux also show, is the truth of a certain refusal of sense and of coherence within a closed and thematically sufficient form.

This imbrication of opposites that the comic implies accounts for two puzzling aspects of jokes and of the humorous tale. That is, their apparent gratuity and their essentially resolved form.

As we have seen, comedy produces the feeling of "having always already known." The economy of the comic story is persistently symmetrical since at the end the reader or listener has the feeling of returning to the beginning. "Du Preudom qui rescolt son compere de noier," for example, is the tale of a fisherman who, in rescuing a drowning colleague, accidentally blinds him in one eye. Like B. in Freud's kettle joke, the ingrate sues ("Cist vilains m'a mon ueil crevé, / Et ge ne l'ai de riens grevé" [*Recueil*, I, 301]); only here the judge rules that:

> Cil preudons, qui conta avant,
> Soit arriers en la mer mis,
> La où cil le feri en vis,
> Que, se il s'en puet eschaper,
> Cil li doit oeil amender;
> C'est droit jugemenz, ce me samble.
>
> (*Recueil*, I, 303)

The plaintiff should be put back into the sea right in the place where the defendant hit him in the eye; and if he can escape, the defendant must compensate him for his loss of sight; this is a judicious decision if ever I saw one.

Once the blindness of the joke-work's initial premise has been removed, the comic tale returns to a *status ante quem* which contains in germ all that has followed. Put another way, the joke or tale projects a pervasive sense of its own gratuity. The joke seems to say that it might have spared the listener the trouble had he been able to listen intelligently at the outset.

Whereas tragedy seems to proceed from necessity, from exigencies imposed either by the gods or by inner psychic reality, comedy is always somewhat gratuitous—undetermined, *de trop*, a surplus added to an already complete universe. This is why desire in the fabliaux so often appears excessive and those who experience it greedy; why chance plays such a large role in their dramatic development; why the fabliau appears to come from nowhere, unmotivated except by the desire for a tale; and why, finally, neither the joke nor the comic tale leaves any excess—any residue of energy or meaning—despite its always excessive status.

Unlike the epic which is transcendent and cyclical and unlike the romance which is continuous and in certain cases (e.g., *Perceval*) interminable, the fabliaux offer a quick fix. They are short and dirty; but they clean up their own mess, and they never leave any loose ends. For example, "De l'Enfant qui fu remis au soleil," a tale which exists in numerous Latin and vernacular versions, contains the story of a merchant whose wife explains that the child born during his prolonged absence was conceived by a "bit of snow that got into her mouth." The merchant patiently waits until the son is old enough to travel, departs for the Middle East where he sells him into slavery, and then explains to his wife how the "snow-child" melted: "Que vos fil remetre covint / De l'ardeur qui du soleil vint" (*Recueil*, I, 166). The child born to the absent merchant is superfluous by definition; but this excessiveness is only redoubled by that of the wife's explanation and by the husband's invention. Together the fictions within the fiction point to the redundancy of the comic enterprise, as the return to the *status ante quem* is transformed into the equivalent of a natural law, that is, "What A does to B, B (or C) will do to A." "De l'Enfant" is thus a tale of superfluousness and liquidation that ends where it began: "Bien l'en avint qu'avenir dut / Qu'ele brassa ce qu'ele but" (*Recueil*, I, 167). And it is in this respect an ideal illustration of the humorous tale as a paradoxical dissipation of that which it invents.

All of which points to a response to the question of what the joke hides—which is precisely the possibility of any univocal determination of its own status. In its displacements, condensations, and substitutions, the joke disrupts the assumption of a "natural" relation between language and meaning and, at the same time, serves as a screen for the fact that such a relation never existed in the first place. Again like the fabliaux, jokes are dirty not because they speak obscenely of hostile deeds or are wickedly antisocial, but because they threaten to expose the scandalous relation of language to an unlocalizable, undefinable, insubstantial point of origin.[36] As Freud acknowledges, they come from nowhere and cover an absence: "We have an undefinable feeling, rather, which I can best compare with an 'absence,' a sudden release of intellectual tension, and then all at once the joke is there—as a rule ready-clothed in words" (*JU*, p. 167).

This impossibility of determinancy, of saying univocally what the comic is, makes it serious—even dangerous. For what is at stake is the very kind of distinction found above, that is, between the joke and its "ready-made" clothing, or, as Freud puts it elsewhere, between the substance or the nucleus (*Kern*) of the joke and its envelope or form (*Hülle*) (*JU*, p. 92). Put another way, the joke, like the impertinent child in "The Emperor's New Clothes," risks exposing the inessential—fictive, conventional—status of the difference between inner and outer, just as the psychoanalytic description of the process of fetishism, like all theoretical thinking of which it is the model, risks collapsing the difference between the Self and the Other. Both fetishism and the comic serve to legitimize the very principle of difference which they call radically into question. Ultimately, their proximity enables us, like the Jongleur of Ely, to turn the King of England's inquiry with which we began back upon him. The questions posed in the course of the chance encounter at the crossroads, and having to do with the origin, identity, and destination of the Other, are those which have to do more properly with his own being. And the poet's comic answers to the king's desire for oedipal knowledge give us reason, finally, to wonder (and we are not the first) whether the joke is oedipal in structure or the Oedipus complex is a joke.[37]

NOTES

ABBREVIATIONS

All translations of French sources are the author's.

Contes orientaux	G. Paris, *Les Contes orientaux dans la littérature française du moyen âge* (Paris: A. Francke, 1875).
Contribution	J. Rychner, *Contribution à l'étude des fabliaux* (Geneva: Droz, 1960).
De Planctu	Alain de Lille, *De Planctu Naturae* in *Patrologia Latina*, ed. J.-P. Migne (Paris: Garnier, 1879), vol. 210.
De Planctu	Alain de Lille, *The Plaint of Nature*, trans. James J. Sheridan, (Toronto: Pontifical Institute of Medieval Studies, 1980).
Erec	Chrétien de Troyes, *Erec et Enide*, ed. M. Roques (Paris: Champion, 1963).
Etat	J. B. B. de Roquefort-Flaméricourt, *De l'Etat de la poésie françoise dans les XIIe et XIIIe siècles* (Paris: Fournier, 1815).
FA	Le Grand d'Aussy, *Fabliaux ou contes du XIIe et du XIIIe siècle* (Paris: Eugène Onfroy, 1781).
"Fabliaux"	F. Brunetière, "Les Fabliaux du moyen âge et l'origine des contes," *Revue des Deux Mondes* 119 (1893): 189–213.
Fabliaux et contes	E. Barbazan, *Fabliaux et contes* (Paris: Crapelet, 1808).
FB	J. Bédier, *Les Fabliaux: Etudes de littérature populaire et d'histoire littéraire du moyen âge* (Paris: Champion, 1925).
FL	V. LeClerc, *Les Fabliaux* in *Histoire littéraire de la France* (Paris: H. Welter, 1895), vol. 23.
FM	P. Ménard, *Les Fabliaux: Contes à rire du moyen âge* (Paris: Presses Universitaires de France, 1984).
FN	P. Nykrog, *Les Fabliaux: Etude d'histoire littéraire et de stylistique médiévale* (Copenhagen: Munksgaard, 1957).

Façons	M.-T. Lorcin, *Façons de sentir et de penser les fabliaux français* (Paris: Champion, 1978).
"Fetishism"	S. Freud, "Fetishism" in *Collected Papers*, ed. J. Strachey (New York: Basic Books, 1959), 5:198–204.
JU	S. Freud, *Jokes and their Relation to the Unconscious* (New York: Norton, 1960).
Mémoire	M. le Comte de Caylus, *Mémoire sur les fabliaux* (Paris: Académie Royale des Inscriptions et Belles Lettres, 1753).
Recueil	A. de Courde de Montaiglon, *Recueil général et complet des fabliaux* (Paris: Librairie des Bibliophiles, 1872–90).
"Richeut"	I. C. Lecompte, ed., "Richeut," *Romanic Review* 4 (1913):263–305.
Rose	Guillaume de Lorris and Jean de Meun, *Le Roman de la rose*, ed. D. Poirion (Paris: Flammarion, 1974).
Silence	L. Thorpe, ed., *Le Roman de Silence* (Cambridge: W. Heffer, 1972).
Trubert	G. Renaud de Lage, ed., *Trubert* (Geneva: Droz, 1974).

INTRODUCTION

1. Whoever produced the manuscript was aware of this connection, since an inscription at the top of Harley ms. 2253, fol. 107v° reads: "Cy comence le flabel du Jongleur de Ely et de monseigneur le roy d'Engleterre, lequel jongleur dona conseil al roi pur sei amender e son Estat garder." The text is to be found in *Recueil*, II, 242.

2. M. le Comte de Caylus, *Mémoire*, p. 355.

3. *Calilah et Dimnah, ou Fables de Bidpaï en arabe. Mémoire sur l'origine de ce livre, et sur les divers traductions qui ont été faites dans l'Orient* (Paris: Imprimerie Royale, 1816), p. 8.

4. T. Benfey, *Pantchatantra* (Leipzig: F. U. Brodhaus, 1859), p. 24.

5. G. Paris, *Contes orientaux*, p. 6; see also Benfey, *Pantchatantra* p. xxvi.

6. "Through Persian, Arabian, Rabbinic versions, these collections reached Europe, where they found entrance to the Middle Latin literature both from the east through the Greek, and by another and direct course." B. Ten Brink, *Early English Literature* (New York: Henry Holt and Company, 1889), I:178.

7. J. and W. Grimm, *Kinder- und Hausmärchen* (Berlin:

G. Reimer, 1856); A. Kuhn, *Die Herabkunft des Feuers und des Gottertranks* (Berlin: F Dümmler, 1859); M. Bréal, *Mélanges de mythologie et de linguistique* (Paris: Hachette, 1882); M. Müller, *Essais sur la mythologie comparée* (Paris: Didier, 1873).

8. Müller, *Essais*, p. 271.

9. M. Müller, "The Last Results of the Researches Respecting the Non-Iranian and Non-Semitic Languages of Asia or Europe, or the Turanian Family of Language," in *Outline of the Philosophy of Universal History*, edited by C. C. J. Bunsen (London: Longman, Brown, Green, and Longman, 1854), I:281.

10. Benfey, *Pantchatantra*, p. 26.

11. Petrus Alfonsi, "Letter on Study" in the *Disciplina clericalis* (Berkeley: University of California Press, 1977), p. 41.

12. Le Grand d'Aussy explains: "C'est sur-tout par ce tableau si intéressant des moeurs & du costume de leur tems, plus encore que par quelques beautés particulieres, que pourront plaire les Fabliaux. Et ce ne sont point seulement des moeurs générales, ou celles des conditions les plus élevées, qu'ils nous représentent. Faits par leur nature, comme la Comédie, pour peindre les actions ordinaires de la vie privée, ils montrent la Nation en déshabille, s'il est permis de parler ainsi. Opinions, préjugés, superstitions, coutumes, ton de conversation, maniere de faire l'amour, tout se trouve là; & beaucoup de choses ne se trouvent que là. J'ose même croire que quand on les aura lus, on connaîtra mieux les Français du treizieme siecle, que si on lisait toutes nos histoires modernes." FA, p. lxxii.

13. J. B. B. de Roquefort-Flaméricourt, *Etat*, p. 188.

14. It was, in fact, a reading of the fabliaux with this phrase constantly in mind that partially inspired the present essay (see above p. 53).

15. E. Faral, *La Vie quotidienne au temps de Saint Louis* (Paris: Hachette, 1938), p. 48.

16. V. LeClerc, FL, p. 70.

17. See also M. J. Joly, "De la Condition des vilains au moyen âge d'après les fabliaux," *Mémoires de l'Académie Nationale des Sciences, Arts et Belles-Lettres* (Caen: Leblanc-Hardel, 1882), pp. 445–92; Ch. Muscatine, "The Social Background of the Old French Fabliaux," *Genre* 9 (1976): 1–19; O. Patzer, "The Wealth of the Clergy in the Fabliaux," *Modern Language Notes* 19 (1904): 195–96. Patzer concludes that the treatment of the clergy "in these stories is but a faithful picture of their actual condition at that time." For a bibliography of works on the question of social realism see: P. Nykrog, FN, pp. 303–8; Ménard, FM, pp. 246–47.

18. Thus O. Jodogne, affirming how "close they are to historical reality," considers the fabliaux to be "especially accurate" in their portrayal of the rural world, while G. Bianciotto places them in a "specifically urban context" and A. Vàrvaro urges careful distinction between the "fabliaux *contadini*" and the "fabliaux *cittadini*," O. Jodogne, *Le Fabliau* (Brepolis: Turnhout, 1975), p. 26; "à mon sentiment, le fabliau s'inscrit très souvent dans une problématique liée à un cadre de vie d'une part, à des structures sociales et familiales de l'autre, qui délimite un contexte spécifiquement urbain," G. Bianciotto, "Le Fabliau et la ville," *Third International Beast Epic, Fable and Fabliau Colloquium* (Köln: Böhlan Verlag, 1981), p. 43; A. Vàrvaro, "I *Fabliaux* e la società," *Studi Mediolatini e Volgari* 8 (1960):287.

19. M.-T. Lorcin, *Façons*, p. 126.

20. I cannot resist quoting this one at some length: "Comme le personnage est qualifié du terme de *asnier*, on a l'impression d'avoir affaire à quelqu'un qui ne remplit pas cette tâche épisodiquement, pour améliorer le rendement de ses propres champs, mais à un véritable spécialiste habitué au transport de matières malodorantes. L'auteur du conte le présente comme un familier de l'ordure. Nous n'avons pas les moyens de mettre en doute ses dires" (FM, p. 52).

21. Bréal, *Mélanges*, p. 3 (see note 7). For Bréal, in fact, the quest for origins is the direct corollary of the denial of interpretation. The passage cited continues: "la seule manière de l'expliquer, c'est de remonter, à travers la série de ses métamorphoses, jusqu'à son origine, et d'en écrire l'histoire," (p. 4).

22. J. Rychner, "Les Fabliaux: Genre, Styles, Publics" in *La Littérature narrative d'imagination* (Paris: Presses Universitaires de France, 1961), p. 51.

23. G. Paris, *Contes orientaux*, p. 20. The positing of a nonpoetic poetics, which contrasts with the romantic adoption of the literature of chivalry as a literature of ideals and of idealism, was a function of the naturalist impulse to escape idealism and ideology which were associated with poetry itself.

24. J. Bédier, FB, p. 341.

25. Brunetière, "Fabliaux," p. 192. Brunetière, in fact, went much further: "If," he advises, "you want to discover what is of specifically literary value in the medieval tale, do not bother learning the language; read Rabelais, Lafontaine, and reread Molière." Brunetière, "L'érudition contemporaine et la littérature française du moyen âge," in *Etudes critiques sur l'histoire de la littérature française* (Paris: Hachette, 1888), p. 50. Here is a good example of the commonly held prejudice that manner was the invention of Renaissance and neoclassical writers who, Brunetière asserts, "submitted the fabliaux to the rules of composition, the laws of style" (p. 49).

26. Le Grand d'Aussy, FA, p. lxxiv.

27. For a discussion of this topic see my *Etymologies and Genealogies: A Literary Anthropology of the French Middle Ages* (Chicago: University of Chicago Press, 1983), pp. 44–63.

28. Gustave Lanson, whose disdain for medieval literature took the form of neglect, speaks of "cette copieuse spontanéité du prosaïsme bourgeois qui sort (faut-il s'en féliciter?) du plus intime fond de la race," Lanson, *Histoire Illustrée de la littérature française* (Paris: Hachette, 1923), I:72. And in a move not devoid of a little ethnocentrism, he attributes France's victory over Germany in World War I to the nonidealistic essence of "l'esprit gaulois": "La forme inférieure du type français c'est l'esprit gaulois. . . . Il s'attaque moins aux grandes choses qu'aux grand mots, aux prétentions qui s'étalent, et à l'idéalisme de façade. . . ." (p. 9).

29. De Caylus, *Mémoire*, p. 356; "que deviendra l'Italie, qui nous a si souvent & si long-temps battus avec nos propres armes, c'est-à-dire, avec nos idées, & les mots qu'elle a pris de nous pour former sa langue? L'Italie, dis-je, qui se glorifie avec raison d'avoir produit Bocace & quelques autres de ses conteurs, perdroit beaucoup de son avantage, si on rendoit publics ces anciens manuscrits François" (p. 375).

30. De Caylus, *Mémoire*, p. 356; Le Grand d'Aussy, FA, p. lxvii; ". . . nul, on peut le dire, ne leur a contesté le naturel, la facilité, la clarté, l'enjouement, l'esprit vif et libre, qui, sans être des qualités sublimes, n'ont pas cessé depuis, à divers degrés et sous diverses formes, de recommander aux autres nations le théâtre, l'apologue, les romans, les journaux français," LeClerc, FL, p. 79; see also L. Lesouds, *L'Esprit gaulois au moyen âge* (Paris: P. Sevin, 1908).

31. Thus, for example, LeClerc's assimilation of low social status, base behavior, and the "low style": "Aussi vient-on de voir que dans les rôles assignés à chaque classe . . . les vilains passent généralement pour fidèles à cette grossièreté brutale que leur reconnaissent leurs meilleurs amis entre les trouvères. De là tant de sales histoires qu'on met sur leur compte, et dont quelques-unes paraissent l'oeuvre des derniers des vilains . . . ; comme ce honteux poëme d'*Audigier*, parodie repoussante des romans chevaleresques, et tant d'autres 'vilenies' que nous ne pouvons même indiquer." LeClerc, FL, p. 204.

32. Bédier actually suggests such a move, though he (intentionally?) lets it drop: "Il semble donc qu'il y ait, au XIIIe siècle, jusqu'à un certain point, confusion des genres et promiscuité des publics." Bédier, FB, p. 384.

33. J. Rychner, *Contribution*, p. 145. A major difficulty with Rychner's thesis, it seems, is the trickiness of defining an aristocratic or bourgeois sensibility or esthetic as necessitated by his claims.

34. Thus too Vàrvaro (who must have known Rychner's work though his article appeared slightly earlier): "la conclusione di questo nostro esame sembra essere del tutto negativa: il publico dei *fabliaux* è risultato privo de caratterizzazione sociale" Vàrvaro, "I *Fabliaux* e la società," p. 298.

35. See LeClerc, FL, pp. 103–4; E. Faral, *Mimes français du XIIIe siècle* (Paris: Champion, 1910), p. 74.

36. LeClerc, FL, p. 98.

37. Doubts about the genre as a genre are inherent in Max Luthi's articulation of the fabliaux as the "possibility of every genre," Luthi, *Märchen* (Stuttgart: Metzler, 1968), p. 13; or in Nykrog's assertion that "the corpus of the fabliaux is so heterogeneous that scarcely any formula applies to the whole," Nykrog, "Courtliness and the Townspeople: The Fabliaux as Courtly Burlesque" in *The Humor of the Fabliaux*, ed. T. D. Cooke and B. L. Honeycutt (Columbia: University of Missouri Press, 1974), p. 71. See also P. Dronke, "The Rise of the Medieval Fabliau: Latin and Vernacular Evidence," *Romanische Foreschungen* 85, no. 3 (1973):275.

38. LeClerc, for example, goes no further, in his "official" presentation of the fabliaux, than presenting a series of resumés of the plots of the various tales.

39. See also Ménard, FM, pp. 104, 107.

CHAPTER I

1. This, in fact, is also an Arthurian motif: ". . . toutes les fois que ie porterai corone iou veu a dieu que ia ne serrai al mangier devant que aucune auenture i sera auenue de quel part ke che soit." (". . . for as long as I am king I swear to God that I will not sit down to eat until some adventure will have happened, from no matter where.") "L'estoire de Merlin" in *The Vulgate Version of the Arthurian Romances*, ed. O. Sommer (Washington: Carnegie Institute, 1908), II:320.

2. See P. Richter, "Versuch einer Dialektbestimmung des Lai du Corn und das Fabliau de Mantel Mautaillé," *Ausgaben und Abhandlung aus dem Gebiete der Romanischen Philologie* 38 (1885); T. P. Cross, "Notes on the Chastity-Testing Horn and Mantle," *Modern Philology* 10 (1913):293–94.

3. Ambrosii Theodosii Macrobii, *Commentarii in Somnium Scipionis*, ed. J. Willis (Leipzig: Teubner, 1970), pp. 7–8. Trans. W. H. Stahl.

4. Chrétien de Troyes, *Erec*, v. 6671.

5. On the relation between economic and linguistic property see my *Etymologies and Genealogies: A Literary Anthropology of the French*

Middle Ages (Chicago: University of Chicago Press, 1983), pp. 40, 51–52.

6. Erec to his future father-in-law: "Iluec vos donrai deus chastiax, / molt boens, molt riches, et molt biax; / sires seroiz de Roadan, / qui fu fez des le tans Adan, / et d'un autre chastel selonc / qui ne valt mie moins un jonc; / la gent l'apelent Montrevel, / mon peres n'a meillor chastel. / Einz que troi jor soient passez / vos avrai anvoié assez / or et argent et veir et gris / et dras de soie et de chier pris / por vos vestir et vostre fame. . . ." ("There [in my land] I will give you two very good, rich, and beautiful castles. You will be lord of Roadan, which was built in Adam's time, and of another castle nearby, which is not worth a farthing less; people call it Montrevel. My father has no better castle. And before three days are up I will have sent to you enough gold and silver and fine cloth and furs and expensive silk to clothe you and your wife. . . .") *Erec,* v. 1317.

7. "Quant Erec sa fame reçut / par son droit non nomer l'estut, / qu'altrement n'est fame esposee, / se par son droit non n'est nomee. / Ancor ne savoit l'an son non, / mes ore primes le set l'on: / Enyde ot non au baptestire." ("When Erec wed his wife it behooved him to call her by her proper name, for otherwise a wife is not wed, unless she is named by her proper name. Until that time, one did not know her name, but henceforth one knew it: she received the name Enide at the baptismal font.") *Erec,* v. 1973.

8. M. Zink, *La Chanson de Toile* (Paris: Champion, 1978), p. 93; see also pp. 96, 130, 161.

9. Ibid., p. 77.

10. "At these words and this thought her love entered the house" (*Idem*).

11. "Vez, fet il, biaus amis Nicole, / quel ovriere il a en ma dame. / C'est une mervellouse fame / et set assez de cest mestier. / Fanons, garnemenz de moustier, chasubles, beles aubes parees, / ont amdeus maintes foiz ouvres." ("You see, he said, good friend Nicole, what a fine weaver my lady is. She is a marvellous woman and knows much about this craft. Both [she and my sister] have worked many times on liturgical and monastic garments, chasubles, and beautiful decorated collars.") Jean Renart, *Guillaume de Dole,* ed. F. Lecoy (Paris: Champion, 1962), v. 1130.

12. See *Guillaume de Dole,* vv. 1178–1192; Zink, *Chanson de Toile,* pp. 3–5, 158.

13. *Biographies des troubadours,* ed. J. Boutière and A.-H. Schutz (Paris: Nizet, 1964).

14. "Her dress, woven from silk-smooth wool, kaleidoscopic in its various colors, served the purpose of a robe of office for the maiden." De Planctu, p. 85.

15. Guillaume de Lorris and Jean de Meun, *Rose*, v. 59.

16. See *Rose*: "Cote avoit viés et derompue" (v. 208); "N'el n'avoit pas sa robe chiere, / ains l'ot en mains leus desciree" (v. 316); "Tant seüst sa robe vendre, / Qu'ele ere nue comme vers" (v. 444).

17. See *Etymologies and Genealogies*, pp. 138–41.

18. On the fabliaux as a "countergenre," see Ch. Muscatine, "The Social Background of the Old French Fabliaux," *Genre* 9 (1976):1–19.

19. It should be noted that though I do not explore the issue here, the representation of representation as always inherently inadequate and the representation of representation as a coat are no less present in theological tradition. For further reference to this subject, see the magisterial *Exégèse médiévale: Les quatre sens de l'écriture* of Henri de Lubac (Paris: Aubier, 1959), especially I, pt. 1, pp. 119–28.

20. "Some laugh in the morning who cry at night; and cry at night who laugh in the morning" (*Recueil*, IV, 91).

21. "Si com tu as mençonge dite! / Te preigne male mort soubite. / Brifaut, vos l'avez brifaudée, / Car fust or la langue eschaudée / Et la gorge par où passerent / Li morsel qui si chier costerent; / Bien vos devroit en devorer" (*Recueil*, IV, 152). ("What a lie you've told! You deserve a sudden nasty death. Brifaut, you have gobbled it up. And may the tongue and the throat down which slid such expensive fare burn; and may it consume you.")

22. "She gained more by her treachery and her lying than those who take, and steal and rob." "Richeut," v. 366.

23. "Par la parole / Fu Sansonez mis a escole. / Mout ot cler sans, / N'ot si sotil en toz les rans: / Son sautier sot en po de tans / Chanta .II. anz. / Voiz ot sor les autres enfanz, / Mout sot et conduiz et sochanz. / Vait a gramaire, / E .I. en sot bien ditié faire. / Con plus aprant et plus esclaire / Tant a fait vers / Qu'il en set faire divers." ("In order to learn to speak well Sanson was sent to school. He was so clearheaded there was not a more subtle mind in the class. He knew his psalter in short order and sang it in two years; his voice carried over the other children, and he could do both lead and chorus. He studied grammar and learned how to make rhymes. The more he learned, the more poems he did, since he knew how to make different kinds.") "Richeut," v. 555.

24. See *Etymologies and Genealogies*, pp. 133–41; R. Dragonetti, "Renart est mort, Renart est vif, Renart règne," *Critique* 375–76 (1978):783–98; E. Vance, "Désire, rhétorique et texte," *Poétique* 42 (1980):137–55.

25. "There the eagle, assuming first the form of a youth, secondly that of an old man, thirdly returning to his former state, makes his way back from Nestor to Adonis" (De Planctu, p. 86); "There the

phoenix dead in himself, brought to life again in another phoenix, by some miracle of nature raised himself from the dead by his death" (De Planctu, p. 88).

26. "There the marten and the sable, by the excellence of their skins, brought to perfection the imperfect beauty of the mantles that called for their help" (De Planctu, p. 104).

27. "These living things, though they had there a kind of figurative existence, nevertheless seemed to live there in the literal sense" (De Planctu, p. 94).

28. "There the parrot fashioned on the anvil of his throat a mint for human speech. There the quail, failing to recognize the deception in the inflection of speech, was deceived by the trickery of an imitative voice" (De Planctu, p. 32).

29. Gautier de Coinci, "Seinte Léocade" in Barbazan, *Fabliaux et contes*, I:v. 1232.

30. "Far vos a de gossa can / Et d'eyssa guiza levar / Lo dia tro l'endeman. . . ." *Les Poésies de Bernart Marti*, ed. E. Hoepffner (Paris: Champion, 1929), p. 5.

31. "S'uns hom en hermitage habite, / C'il est de povres draz vestus, / Je ne pris mie .III. festus / Son habit ne sa vesteüre, / C'il ne mainne vie ausi pure / Conme ces habiz nos demoustre" (*Recueil*, III, 263). ("If a man lives in a hermitage and if he is dressed in poor clothes, I do not respect either his life or clothing if he does not also lead a life as pure as his clothes show.")

32. "He who should have made her understand the meaning of her lesson instead placed her in evil straits" (*Recueil*, III, 266); "Ces biaus crins a fait reoignier, / Comme vallez fu estanciée, / Et fu de boens houziaus chauciée, / Et de robe à home vestue, / Qui estoit par devant fendue" (*Recueil*, III, 267). ("This beautiful mane was tonsured; and she was changed into a man, shoed in fine hose and dressed in a man's garb that was open in front.")

33. "Nature, who inscribed her ears, made them small and the brows brown and well placed. No one could imagine a prettier one." *Silence*, v. 1917. The function of Nature is to create difference which is insured by names: "Molles i a bien .m. milliers, / Que cho li est moult grans mestiers, / Car s'ele n'eüst formé c'une / Sa samblance estoit si commune / De tolte gent, c'on ne savroit / Quoi, ne quel non, chascuns avroit. / Mais Nature garda si bien / En s'uevre n'a a blasmer rien." ("She had at least a thousand thousand moulds, for she had great need. Indeed, if she had formed only one, her semblance would be so common that one could not tell what name everyone should have. But Nature took care, and in her work there is nothing to blame.") *Silence*, v. 1887.

34. "Secrétés par les pays de langue d'oïl, les fabliaux ne dépay-

sent pas leur public. Leur univers s'étend de la Loire à l'Escaut. . . .
Les lieux où l'action est située forment sur la carte un semis très serré
en Hainaut, patrie du jongleur Gautier Le Leu, en Flandre, Picardie
et Normandie. Les points sont plus espacés en Champagne et dans le
Chartrain, plus encore en Bourgogne et en Angleterre." M.-Th.
Lorcin, *Façons*, p. 7.

35. "Or tien, fet il, cest mantel gris, / certes, qu'il est bien em-
ploiez. . . . / Par Jouglet, cui il ot partie / sa robe as chans, fist apeler
/ un clerc, si le fist aporter / encre, parchemin et l'afere / quë il co-
vient a letres fere. / Tuit troi vont en la garde robe; / Jouglet de sa cote
le robe / dont il avoit ja le mantel." ("Now take this grey mantle; it is
certainly put to good use. . . . Through Jouglet, to whom he already
gave his robe, he had a cleric called and had him bring ink, paper,
and all that is necessary to write letters. The three of them go into the
wardrobe room; Jouglet, who already had the mantle, robbed him of
the coat.") *Guillaume de Dole*, vv. 723, 868.

36. "C'apartient à ces jougleors, / Et à ces bons enchanteors, /
Que il aient des chevaliers / Les robes, que c'est lor mestiers" (*Re-
cueil*, III, 42).

37. "Jamais, à nul jor, robe nueve / N'a u, pour chose que il die"
(*Recueil*, I, 2); "Je t'ai veü par maintes cors / Que tu n'avoies pas vestu
/ Vaillant .III. solz. / Mès qui es tu?" (II, 259); "Ne n'es tu pas de grant
renon / Si comme autre menestrel sont / Qui aus granz cors les robes
ont" (II, 262).

38. "Ne deüsses pas avoir cote / Qui fust entiere? mès la hote /
Ce deüst estre tes mestiers, / Et fien porter en .II. paniers" (*Recueil*,
II, 258).

39. "Know that one does not shit the day one marries his be-
trothed, for that would be too gross a thing to do" (*Recueil*, IV, 115).

40. V. LeClerc, in fact, equates Jouglet's fate with a certain "moral
lesson": "Jouglet . . . est odieusement sali de la tête aux pieds pen-
dant son sommeil. . . . L'impudent auteur . . . n'en tire pas moins de
la mésaventure de Jouglet une leçon morale." FL, p. 206.

41. "Ses peres tint Cocuce un païs mou, / Où les gens sont en
merde jusqu'au cou: / Par un ruissel de foire m'en ving à non, / On-
ques n'en poi issir par autre trou." Barbazan, *Fabliaux et contes*,
IV:217.

42. "Audigier prist la Dame par le mantel, / . . . En chiant li a
mis el doi l'ennel" (*Fabliaux et contes*, IV:232); "Puis ont éu après un
bon civé / De merde de geline entremellé" (*Idem.*); "Il i ot jugléors
bien jusqu'à cent, / Lendemain sont venus au paiement, / Et Audigier
lor donne molt liéement, / Trente crotes de chievre à chascun tent"
(*Fabliaux et contes*, IV, 233).

43. "Et li vilains, qui se degrate, / Apoinge sa coille et son vit; / Sa fame apele que il vit: / Suer, fet il, foi que moi devez, / Or devinez, se vous savez, / Que c'est que je tieng en mon poing?" (Recueil, III, 46).

44. "La dame trestout coiement / Taste à son cul isnelement, / Si a trové une crote / Qui resamble une machelot / Qui estoit plus grosce d'un pois" (Recueil, III, 47).

45. M. A. Joly writes, just to cite one example that is very much à propos: "Le vilain est immonde en ses gaîtés. Voyez-le tel que nous le présente le fabliau de la Crotte, le soir se reposant du labeur du jour, assis au coin de son maigre foyer, face à face avec sa vilaine, aussi misérable et repoussante que lui, faisant avec elle assaut de grossier propos. Quand le vilain veut faire une niche à sa femme, le français, celui même de l'école odurist en honneur aujourd'hui, oserait difficilement dire ce qu'il peut trouver sur lui pour lui donner à goûter et à deviner"—Joly is confused about who tastes what. "De la Condition des vilains au moyen âge d'après les fabliaux," Mémoires de l'Académie Nationale des Sciences, Arts et Belles-Lettres (Caen: Leblanc-Hardel, 1882), p. 29. V. LeClerc describes "De la Crote" as a fabliau "qu'on aurait bien pu se dispenser d'imprimer tout entière," (FL, p. 206).

46. Even her husband's wonderment at where she "found it" ("Que où que soit avez trovée") can be understood in these terms.

47. In Recueil, see also: **I**, 70, 178, 255; **II**, 49, 171, 178, 264; **III**, 1, 30, 51, 54, 88, 106, 186, 209, 247, 252, 275; **IV**, 46, 47, 53, 127, 212; **V**, 32, 64, 95, 101, 132, 160, 171, 179, 184, 191, 244; **VI**, 42, 50, 68, 117, 138.

48. Ménard, FM, pp. 151, 161.

49. The attempt to "cleanse" the scandal of the fabliaux has, in fact, a long tradition stretching all the way back to Le Grand d'Aussy's promise to make them decent enough for polite society: "Il est des Contes licencieux que je supprimerai en entier; il en est que je ne présenterai qu'en extrait, ou dont je retrancherai les détails trop libres. Ce n'est point là dépouiller un Auteur; c'est le mettre en état d'entrer chez les honnêtes-gens." FA, p. lxxvii.

50. "Si t'aït Diex, où emblas tu / Cel sorcot que tu as vestu?" (Recueil, II, 261).

51. "Si sai bien faire frains à vaches / Et ganz à chiens, coifes à chièvres. / Si sai faire haubers à lièvres, / Si forz qu'il n'ont garde de chiens" (Recueil, I, 5).

52. "Ge suis cil qui les maisons cuevre / D'ués friz, de torteax en paele; / Il n'a home jusqu'à Neele / Qui mielz les cuevre que ge faz. / Ge sui bons seignerres de chaz, / Et bons ventousierres de bués; / Si

sui bons relierres d'ués, / Li mieldres qu'en el monde saaiches"
(*Idem.*)

53. "Si faz bien forreax à trepiez / Et bones gaïnes à sarpes, / Et se
ge avoie .II. harpes, / Ge nel lairai que ne vos die, / Ge feroie une
meloudie / Ainz ne fu oïe si grantz" (*Recueil*, I, 5–6).

54. "De pluzors sens / Sui ples e prens / De cent colors per miells
chauzir; / Fog porti sai / Et augua lai, / Ab que sai la flam' escantir."
Les Poésies de Marcabru, ed. J. Dejeanne (Paris: Champion, 1909),
p. 67. See *Etymologies and Genealogies*, pp. 108–27.

55. "Et fant los motz, per esmanssa, / Entrebeschatz de frai-
chura" (*Les Poésies de Marcabru*, p. 178); "Cars, bruns et tenhz
motz entrebesc," W. T. Pattison, ed., *The Life and Works of Raimbaut
d'Orange*, (Minneapolis: University of Minnesota Press, 1952), p. 75.

56. "C'aisi vauc entrebescant / Los motz . . ." Bernart Marti,
Poésies, p. 11.

57. "Farai un vers, pos mi sonelh, / E·m vauc e m'estauc al
solelh." A. Jeanroy, ed., *Les Chansons de William IX*, (Paris: Cham-
pion, 1913), p. 8.

CHAPTER 2

1. *Etymologies and Genealogies: A Literary Anthropology of the
French Middle Ages* (Chicago: University of Chicago Press, 1983),
pp. 137–49.

2. "He cut off the ass and the cunt and put it in his sack . . .
'Lord,' he said, 'here is the mouth and nostrils of Goulias'." *Trubert*,
vv. 1927, 1968.

3. "El dormi, vos di sanz mançonge. / Que la dame sonja un
songe / Qu'ele ert à un marchié anuel, / Ainz n'oïst parler de tel,/
Ainz n'i ot estal ne bojon / Ne n'i ot loge ne maison, / Changes, ne
tables, ne repair / O l'an vandist ne gris ne vair, / Toile de lin, ne drax
de laine, / Ne alun, ne bresil, ne graine, / Ne autre avoir, ce li ert vis, /
Fors solemant coilles o viz" (*Recueil*, V, 186–87). ("In her sleep, I tell
you without a lie, that lady dreamed a dream that she was at a yearly
fair. She had never heard talk of such a one, for there were no stalls
nor yard sticks, no booths nor houses, no change counters nor
tables, nor place where one sold cheap or expensive cloth, neither
linen nor wool, nor alum, nor brazil wood, nor grain, nor other
goods, as it seemed to her, but only balls with cocks.")

4. "Le Fabliau du Moine," ed. A. Långfors, *Romania* 44 (1914):
561.

5. "'Je demant,' dist ele, 'en non Dieu, / Que vous soiez chargiez
de vis. . . . / C'un seul vit ne me valoit rien; / Sempres ert mol
comme pelice'" (*Recueil*, V, 204–5).

6. "Adonc fu ele bien connue / Qu'ele ot .II. cons en la veüe; / .III. en ot ou front cost à cost, / Et con devant et con d'encoste; / Si ot con de mainte maniere / Et con devant et con derriere, / Con tort, con droit et con chenu, / Et con sanz poil et con velu. . . . / Et con parfont et con seur boce, / Et con au chief, et con aus piez" (*Recueil*, V, 206). ("Then she was well covered with cunts since she had two in her eyes, three on her forehead side by side, and a cunt in the front and one on the side. She had cunts of many kinds, both fore and aft: curved cunts, straight cunts, hoary cunts, bald cunts and fuzzy cunts. . . . And deep cunts and cunts on a hump, and cunts on her head and on her feet.")

7. The explanations: 1) "Mes cons si est en bone foi, / Si m'aït Dieus, ainsnez de moi: / Il a barbe, je n'en ai point"; 2) "Sui je ainsnée que mes cons, / Que j'ai les denz et granz et lons, / Et mes cons n'en a encore nus"; 3) "Mes cons est plus jones de moi; / Si vous dirai reson porqoi: / De la mamele sui sevrée, / Mes cons a la goule baée: / Jones est, si veut aletier" (*Recueil*, V, 113–14). (1) "My cunt in good faith is older than me. It has a beard, and I have none"; 2) "I am older than my cunt, since I have teeth both big and long, and my cunt as yet has none"; 3) "My cunt is younger than me, and I will tell you why: I am weaned from the breast, but my cunt has its mouth wide open and still wants to suck.")

8. "Le Dit de soucretain" follows essentially the same plan. See E. B. Vitz, "Desire and Causality in Medieval Narrative," *Romanic Review* 71 (1980):235–43.

9. "Trop me cuidiés mal ensaigniet, / Fil à putain, predome à tort / Qui volés que d'un home mort / Dire ke ce soit uns bacons. . . . / Ne sui mie si enivrés / Que me puissiés à ceste fie / Por lanterne vendre vessie" (*Recueil*, IV, 23); "'Dieus!' dist il, 'c'est cape à provoire / Que je senc chi entre mes mains, / U c'est autre senefiance; . . . / Par mon cief, bacon n'estes mie; / Que diaubles l'eüst vestu?" (IV, 29).

10. "Mais c'est Deable, bien le sai, / Qui a fait moine de bacon" (*Recueil*, V, 236).

11. Thus Thibaut: "Se g'ai le moine dont lier / Ge cuit, g'en ferai chevalier" (*Recueil*, V, 240). ("If I can tie the monk on, I'll make a knight out of him.")

12. The motif of the multiple death is also to be found in the *Huth Merlin* where it is again linked to the multiplicity of semblances that Merlin, another inscription of the poet, provokes. G. Paris and J. Ulrich, eds., *Huth Merlin* (Paris: Firmin Didot, 1886), I:80–84.

13. "If this affair is known, everyone will denounce me" (*Recueil*, IV, 19); "One will say before the abbot that I have killed him treach-

erously" (*Recueil*, V, 230); "One will say that I have killed him" (*Recueil*, IV, 33); "For one will wrongly say that we have killed him for his goods" (IV, 17).

14. See O. Jodogne, *Le Fabliau* (Brepols: Turnhout, 1975), pp. 19–21.

15. "'Mes coutiaus est bien esmolus, / Je le fas ier moudre à la forge, / Ja avra copée la gorge.' / Et quant li prestres l'entendi, / Bien cuida c'on l'eüst trahi: / Du col celui est jus saillis, / Si s'en fuit trestoz esmaris; / Mès son soupeliz ahocha." (*Recueil*, IV, 91).

16. "En la joe un grant cop li frape, / Puis dist: 'Vo buffet et vo nape / Vous rent, ja ne l'en quier porter; / A homme fet mauvès prester / Qui ce ne rent que l'en li preste'" (*Recueil*, III, 204). ("He struck a blow in his face, then said: 'I'm returning your buffet and your napkin, which I don't need anymore. It's not right for a man to borrow what he doesn't give back'.")

17. "'Seignor, dist-il, je ai trové / Là sus .I. erite prové; / Il dist qu'il vous ledengera, / Et si foutera le plus lonc, / Et si batera le plus cort'" (*Recueil*, I, 224–25).

18. "'Mès la robe, que j'aportoie / A la garce, est encore moie: / La dame de ceaus l'aura, / Qui mout meillor gré m'en saura'" (*Recueil*, III, 101). ("'The dress that I brought to that shrew is still in my possession. This lady shall have it, for she will show me greater appreciation'.")

19. See S. M. White, "Sexual Language and Human Conflict in Old French Fabliaux," *Comparative Studies in Society and History* 24 (1982):183–210.

20. "Vint à son proisne sermoner, / Et dist qu'il fesoit bon doner / Por Dieu, qui reson entendoit; / Que Diex au double li rendoit / Celui qui le fesoit de cuer" (*Recueil*, I, 132).

21. Mother to daughter: "Tesiez, fille, ja nule fame, / S'ele n'est se trop male teche, / Ne doit nommer cele peesche / Qui entre les jambes pendeille / A ces hommes" (*Recueil*, V, 102).

22. (*Recueil*, V, 103). Interestingly enough, this passage has been taken by some not as a sign of the denaturing of language but of the "naturalism" of the fabliaux: "It seems to me that this lyrical outburst is as fresh and innocent as its speaker. Part of that force comes from its formalism, its careful use of such rhetorical devices as *repetitio* and *conduplicatio*. . . ." T. D. Cooke, "Pornography, the Comic Spirit, and the Fabliaux" in *The Humor of the Fabliaux*, ed. T. D. Cooke, and B. L. Honeycutt (Columbia: University of Missouri Press, 1974), p. 157.

23. "Lors le commence à reverser / Et toz les fielz à retorner, / Mais jusqu'au jor Ascenssion / N'i trovast il la Passion" (*Recueil*, V, 80).

(Then he began to reverse and to turn all the pages, but from now until Ascension he would not have found the Passion.")

24. "He wanted to speak his mind in French, but the language turned to English, which was no surprise" (*Recueil*, I, 178).

25. *Fabliaux et contes*, IV: 485.

26. "*Pater noster*, biaus sire Diex, / Quar donez que je soie tiex / Que je puisse par mon avoir / Et le los et le pris avoir / De gaaignier et d'amasser / Tant que je puisse sormonter / Trestoz les riches useriers / Qui onques pretaissent deniers. / *Qui es in coelis*, molt me poise / Que je n'i fui quant la borgoise / Voloit emprunter les deniers . . . / *Sanctificetur*, trop me griéve / Que mon argent issi gaster; . . . / *Nomen tuum*. Je claim tout quite / Celui qui envers moi s'acuite; . . . / *Adveniat regnum tuum*. / Retorner vueil à ma meson / Por savoir que ma fame fet." ("*Pater Noster*, please grant that I be such that I can by my money have the power to earn and accumulate so much that I can conquer all the rich usurers who ever lent money. *Qui es in coelis*, it weighs upon me that I was not there when the bourgeoise wanted to borrow deniers. . . . *Sanctificetur*, it hurts me that my maid is so anxious to waste my money here; . . . *Nomen tuum*. I forgive the debts of those who forgive mine; . . . *Adveniat regnum tuum*. I want to go home to see what my wife is doing." (*Fabliaux et contes*, IV: 100ff.); see also the "Credo à l'userier" (IV: 109) and the "Credo au ribaut" (IV: 446).

27. *Fabliaux et contes*, IV: 441–42.

28. "'Biaus amis, car metomes non / A vostre rien et à mon con. . . . / — Sire,' fait el, 'si me plaira / Que mes cons ait non porcelez, / Por ce qu'il ne puet estre nez; / Et vostre rien, ne sai conmant, / Je cuit qu'il avra non fromant, / Car c'est biaus nons'" (*Recueil*, IV, 51).

29. See Jürgen Beyer, "The Morality of the Amoral" in Cooke and Honeycutt, *The Humor of the Fabliaux*, p. 36.

30. "Que en nul sen ne sofrist mie / Sergent qui nomast lecherie: / Vit ne coille ne autre chose. . . . / 'Que, dès que ma fille ot nomer / Foutre, si li prent une gote'" (*Recueil*, V, 25–26).

31. "David, put your beautiful charger in my meadow to graze" (*Recueil*, V, 30).

32. One notable exception to my critique is Roy J. Pearcy's "Modes of Signification and the Humor of Obscene Diction in the Fabliaux" in Cooke and Honeycutt, *The Humor of the Fabliaux*, pp. 59–73.

33. "Quand on a signalé ces quatre mots, un verbe et trois substantifs, on a terminé l'inventaire des mots directement obscènes employés dans les fabliaux." FN, p. 212.

34. "Entre eles .III. Jhesu jurèrent / Que icele l'anel auroit / Qui son mari mieux guileroit / Por fère à son ami son buen, / L'anel auroit et seroit sien" (*Recueil*, I, 168).

35. "In the guise of a monk I will come to her and hear her confession" (*Recueil*, I, 179).

36. "And when it was night he put on the clothes and changed his appearance completely" (*Recueil*, I, 180); "I have been a bad woman, for I gave myself to my serving boys and slept with them" (I, 182).

37. "'Par foi,' fet il, 'ce est la voire, / Puisque je sui hors de la foire, / Et en bon leu, et loing de gent, / Deüsse bien de mon argent / Tout seul par moi savoir la somme; / Ainsi font tuit li sage homme. / J'ai de Rouget .XXXIX. saus, / .XII. deniers en ot Giraus / Qui mes .II. bues m'aida à vendre. / A males forches puist il pendre, / Por ce qu'il retint mes deniers! . . . / J'oi de Sorin .XIX. saus; / De ceus ne fui je mie faus, / Quar mon compere dans Gautiers / Ne m'en donast pas tant deniers / Con j'ai eü de tout le mendre: / Por ce fet bon au marchié vendre; / Il vousist ja creance avoir, / Et j'ai assamblé mon avoir, / .XIX. saus et .XXXIX. / Itant furent vendu mi buef. / Dieus! c'or ne sai que tout ce monte, / Si meïsse tout en .I. conte, / Je ne le savroie sommer; . . . / Et neporquant me dist Sirous / Que j'oi des bues .L. sous, / Qui les conta, si les reçut; / Mès je ne sai s'il m'en deçut, / Ne s'il m'en a neant emblé / Qu'entre .II. sestiers de blé, / Et ma jument et mes porciaus, / Et la laine de mes aigniaus / Me rendirent tout antrestant. / .II. fois .L., ce sont cent, / Ce dis un gars qui fist mon conte; / .V. livres dist que tout ce monte. / Or ne lerai, por nule paine, / Que ma borse qu'est toute plaine, / Ne soit vuidie en mon giron'" (*Recueil*, V, 53–55).

38. "'S'or eüsse ma douce niece, . . . / Dame fust or de mon avoir. . . . / Ahi! douce niece Mabile, / Tant estiiez de bon lingnage, / Dont vous vint ore tel corage? / Or sont tuit troi mort mi enfant, / Et ma fame dame Siersant!'" (*Recueil*, V, 55–56).

39. This is not an uncommon word play. Indeed, "Les .III. Avugles" is a story of false accounts, as is "Du Prestre et du chevalier," a tale of economic dealings which again come to stand for the narrative we are reading (see especially *Recueil*, II, 57–58).

40. So too the mother-in-law at the end of "Du Sot Chevalier": "Ele tout l'afère lor conte; / Si leur a aconté le conte, / Et leur fist savoir et entendre / Que nus hom ne doit sot entendre, / Quar souvent en avient granz maus" (*Recueil*, I, 230). ("She recounted to them the whole matter; she told them the tale. And she let them know in no uncertain terms that one should never listen to a fool, for great ill often comes of it.")

41. "Pappelardie est une trueve / Et une gille toute nueve, / Qui

trovée ont cil guilleur, / Et cil soutil bareteeur / Por demener très soutilement / Leur gille et leur conciement" (*Fabliaux et contes*, I: 319).

42. "Qui menestreil vuet engignier, / Mout en porroit mieulz bargignier; / Car mout souventes avient / Que cil por engignié se tient / Qui menestreil engignier cuide, / Et s'en trueve sa bource vuide" (*Recueil*, III, 222). For a general treatment, see R. Brusegan, "Les Fonctions de la ruse dans les fabliaux," *Strumenti Critici* 47–48 (1982): 148–60.

43. "Richeut," vv. 5, 18, 94, 519; and above p. 36.

44. *Trubert*, vv. 378, 631, 1258.

45. ". . . and Trubert did not hesitate to put on a woman's hood" (*Trubert*, v. 2273); "He (Golias) is completely confounded; he doesn't understand the trick of his wife who has no cunt!" *Trubert*, v. 2790.

46. "'Sire dus, je ai non Trubert. / Bien vos puis tenir por fobert. / Je suis cil qui vous acoupi / et qui la chievre vos vendi / par mon sens, et par mon barnage / vos fis un pertuis en la nage / quant je vos dui le pois sachier; / ersoir fis le pet au mengier / et vostre fame la duchoise / qui est debonaire et cortoise / croissi jë anuit treize fois'" (*Trubert*, v. 827). ("'My Lord and Duke, my name is Trubert. I consider you to be a fool. For I am the one who cuckolded you and sold you the goat by my wit; and by my valor I made you a hole in the ass when I pulled out two hairs. Last night I was the one who farted at dinner; and I fucked your wife, the comely and courtly duchess, thirteen times.'")

47. "No one can know who I am or my name" (*Trubert*, v. 1792); "those who think they know me know nothing of my being" (*Huth Merlin*, I: 68).

1. See FN, pp. 25–38.

2. "'Vous ne porriiez pas trover / Tel non en trestout cest pais. / Bien le vous raconti et devis: / De mes parenz n'i a nul, / J'ai non Berengier au lonc cul; / A trestoz les coars faz honte'" (*Recueil*, IV, 64).

3. "Por ce deffent à toute gent, / Qui se vantent de maint afere / Dont il ne sevent à chief trere, / Qu'il lessent ester lor vantance" (*Recueil*, IV, 66).

4. "Puisque fabloier m'atalante / Et je i ai mise m'entente, / Ne lerai qu'encor ne vous die / Jadis avint en Lombardie. . . ." (*Recueil*, IV, 57).

5. *Fabliaux et contes*, IV: 196.

6. "Que li Cus demandoit au Con / .III. sous de rente qu'il li doit. / Mès li Cons dist que non fesoit, / Qu'il ne l'en doit mie tant /

. . . 'Comment, deable,' dist li Cus, / 'Me veus-tu fere desreson'"
(*Recueil*, II, 133).

7. "Si ot tot le sien despendu . . . / Li chevaliers, en cel termine,
/ Ne li remest mantel d'hermine / Ne surcot, ne chape forrée, / Ne
d'autre avoir une denrée, / Que trestot n'eüst mis en gaige" (*Recueil*,
VI, 69).

8. For this question of medieval "bijoux indiscrets" see A. Leupin,
"Le sexe dans la langue: la dévoration," *Poétique* 45 (1981):91–110.

9. I have purposefully not translated this passage in order to em-
phasize the concrete nature of the poetry rather than its meaning.

10. I. Kant, *Critique of Aesthetic Judgement* (Oxford: Clarendon,
1911), p. 199; G. Meredith, *The Egoist* (Boston: Houghton Mifflin,
1958), p. 7; "All these techniques (of humor) are dominated by a ten-
dency to compression, or rather to saving. It all seems to be a question
of economy. In Hamlet's words: 'Thrift, thrift, Horatio!'" *JU*, p. 42.

11. *JU*, p. 206; R. W. Emerson includes in "The Comic" (1843) a
version of the same story which he reproduces from Samuel Butler's
Hudibras.

12. Freud insists that a joke like that concerning Napoleon III is,
in fact, immune from the nastiness of substitution: "Here no vio-
lence is done to the word; it is not cut up into its separate syllables, it
does not need to be subjected to any modification, it does not have to
be transferred from the sphere it belongs to (the sphere of proper
names, for instance) to another one. Exactly as it is and as it stands in
the sentence, it is able, thanks to certain circumstances, to express
two different meanings" (*JU*, p. 37). Yet the very term which "means
double"—the *vol* that signifies both economic disappropriation and
the displacement of flight—is a tip-off to a linguistic disappropria-
tion operative at an even more basic level. That is, to the extent to
which the word *vol* can mean properly—that is exclusively—both
theft and flight, it radicalizes the entire notion of linguistic property.

13. A. Schopenhauer, *The World as Will and Idea* (London: Trüb-
ner & Co., 1886), II:271.

14. "What on the other hand is inseparable from the comic is an
infinite geneality and confidence capable of rising superior to its own
contradiction. . . ." G. W. F. Hegel, *The Philosophy of Fine Art*,
4 vols. (London: G. Bell and Sons, 1920), 4:302; "Une pensée magi-
que l'a remplacée soudain, moins onéreuse et plus brillante." Ch.
Mauron, *Psychocritique du genre comique* (Paris: José Corti, 1964), p. 39.

15. The reader may be surprised at the ready assimilation of the
fabliaux to jokes, yet because of their essentially verbal wit they are
closer to jokes than any other form of humor. Such an analogy is, in
any case, not unique, for Ch. Mauron asserts of the comic theatre:

". . . une comédie bien construite n'est qu'un vaste et complexe trait d'esprit, savante architecture dont les moellons, à leur tour, peuvent être tenus pour des traits d'esprit élémentaires" (*Psychocritique*, p. 18).

16. And it is the point of the one S. Weber claims to have heard from J. Derrida: "A Jew and a Pole are sitting opposite one another in a train. After some hesitation, the Pole addresses the Jew: 'Itzig, I've always been a great admirer of your people, and especially of your talents in business. Tell me honestly, is there some trick behind it all, something I could learn?' The Jew, after a moment's surprise, replies: 'Brother, you may have something there. But you know, you don't get anything for nothing—it'll cost you.' 'How much?' asks the Pole. 'Five zlotys,' answers the Jew. The Pole nods eagerly, reaches for his wallet and pays the Jew. The latter puts the money away and begins to speak: 'You will need a large whitefish, caught by yourself if possible; you must clean it; pickle it, put it in a jar. . . .' 'And then?' asks the Pole, puzzled, 'Is that all?' 'Not quite,' smiles the Jew in response . . . 'But it will cost you!' The Pole pays, the Jew speaks, and so it goes from Cracow to Lemberg. The Pole grows increasingly impatient, and finally, having paid all his money to the Jew, he explodes: 'You dirty Yid! Do you think I don't know your game?! You take me for a fool, and my money to boot—*that*'s your precious secret!' And the Jew, smiling benignly: 'But Brother, what do you want? Don't you see—it's working already!'" S. Weber, *The Legend of Freud* (Minneapolis: University of Minneapolis Press, 1982), p. 117. Like the Jew on the train, the joke earns its keep by keeping back an awareness of a lack—in this instance the absence of any trick the Pole might learn beyond the limits of the joke itself.

17. Among all those who have written on the fabliaux only Roy J. Pearcy recognizes this opposition to be the essence of their humor: "Instead of a conflict between social classes and their constituent mores and rituals, there emerges from the fabliaux a more profound opposition between an attitude of mind that is essentially speculative, synoptic, and idealistic, and one that is materialistic, analytic and existential." "Modes of Signification and the Humor of Obscene Diction in the Fabliaux" in *The Humor of the Fabliaux*, ed. T. D. Cooke and B. L. Honeycutt (Columbia: University of Missouri Press, 1974), p. 194. My only quibble with Pearcy is that where he considers this conflict to be an expression of the tension between the Augustinian Neoplatonism and the Aristotelianism of the Middle Ages, I consider it to be a more universal principle of humor. But, then again, maybe such philosophical tension is universal.

18. S. Freud, *Standard Edition* (London: Hogarth Press, 1953–56), 7:195.

19. Such a connection is indeed suggested in S. Weber's rereading of Freud. Weber observes, for instance, that the word Freud uses for the dirty joke—*Zote* (from *Zotte*, meaning "unclean hair," "pubic hair," "unclean woman")—is connected etymologically to the female genitalia: "Both the Zote and the shaggy-dog story designate the kind of disreputable, tangled knot that Freud sought either to ignore, in his story of 'castration,' or to describe as the site of something more palpable. . . ." *Legend*, p. 116 (see note 16 above).

20. "Fetishism," p. 198.

21. See M. A. Grant, *The Ancient Rhetorical Theories of the Laughable* (Madison: University of Wisconsin Studies in Language and Literature, 1924), p. 100.

22. See J. Baudrillard, "Fétichisme et idéologie: la réduction sémiologique" in *Objets du fétichisme, Nouvelle Revue de Psychanalyse* 2 (1970):213–26.

23. O. Mannoni, *Clefs pour l'imaginaire* (Paris: Seuil, 1969), p. 12.

24. See S. Freud, "Le Clivage du moi dans le processus de défense" in *Objets du fétichisme*, pp. 25–28; M. Katan, "Fetishism, Splitting of the Ego, and Denial," *International Journal of Psychoanalysis* 45 (1964):241.

25. J.-B. Pontalis, Introduction to *Objets du fétichisme*, p. 11.

26. See, for example: "De la Bourgoise d'Orleans" (I, 22) or "Sire Hain et dam Anieuse" (*Recueil*, I, 110).

27. "'Tesiez vous en,' dist el, 'mauvés, / Gardez que n'en parlez jamès; / Se je vous en oi plus parler, / Le matinet sanz arester, / Ce sachiez vous, sanz atargier / J'irai à seignor Berengier / Au lonc cul, qui a grant poissance: / Bien me fera de vous venjance'" (*Recueil*, IV, 65).

28. "Then she started to hug him, to kiss him, and lick him with her tongue; and she kept her hand on his penis from that day forward" (*Recueil*, III, 74).

29. "Uns riches hom jadis estoit, . . . / Chevaliers ert, tint grant hennor, / Mais tant avoit amé s'ossor, / Que desor lui l'avoit levée, / Et seignoirie abandonée / De sa terre, de sa maison, / Et de tot otroié le don; / Dont la dame le tint si vill / Et tint si bas, que quanque cil / Disoit, et ele desdisoit, / Et deffaisoit quanqu'il faisoit" (*Recueil*, VI, 96). ("There was once a rich man. . . . He was a knight and a man of property; but he loved his wife so much that she gained power over him, and he abdicated his authority over his land and his house, which he gave over. For which reason the lady held him to be so low that whatever he said she gainsaid it, and whatever he did she undid it.")

30. "'Ge vos en faiz asseürance / Que ge ferai quanqu'amerez: / Se nel faz, le chief me tranchiez.' / Ce dist li quens: 'Bele, or sachiez /

Qu'or sofferai, mais se ge voi / Que voilliez reveler vers moi, / Ostez vos seront li coillon, / Si com à vostre mere avon; / Que ce sachiez, par ces grenotes / Sont les femes fieres et sotes'" (*Recueil*, VI, 114).

31. *Clefs*, p. 11.

32. For short summaries of the history of writing on the comic see: J. Feibleman, *In Praise of Comedy* (London: George Allen and Unwin, 1939); P. Lauter, *Theories of Comedy* (New York: Doubleday, 1964).

33. See D. W. Winnicott, "Transitional Objects and Transitional Phenomena: A Study of the First Not-Me Possession," *The International Journal of Psychoanalysis* 34 (1953):89–97; D. W. Winnicott, "The Location of Cultural Experience," *The International Journal of Psychoanalysis* 48 (1966):368–72; Ph. Greenacre, "The Fetish and the Transitional Object," *Psychoanalytic Study of the Child* 24 (1969): 144–64.

34. Mauron, *Psychocritique*, p. 24; Lacan writes, "On voit que la métaphore se place au point précis où le sens se produit dans le non-sens, c'est-à-dire à ce passage dont Freud a découvert que, franchi à rebours, il donne lieu à ce mot qui en français est 'le mot' par excellence, le mot qui n'y a pas d'autre patronage que le signifiant de l'esprit, et où se touche que c'est sa destinée même que l'homme met au défi par la dérision du signifiant." *Ecrits* (Paris: Seuil, 1966), p. 508.

35. *Legend*, p. 114.

36. "The attitudes expressed in the fabliaux are clearly closer to the nominalist position in the nominalist controversy. Ockham's scrupulous separation of physics from metaphysics establishes philosophically the position on which the fabliaux have already taken their stand." Pearcy, "Modes of Signification," p. 195.

37. See Weber, *Legend*, p. 116.

INDEX

EP //

Gramley Library
Salem College
Winston-Salem, NC 27108